Howitzers Grasshoppers and the Holy Right Hand

✯ ✯ ✯ ✯ ✯ ✯ ✯ ✯

The Wartime Experiences Of
Captain Harold E. Brown
United States Army Artillery
World War II

John Niesel

Fort Collins, Colorado

Copyright © 2008 by John Niesel

All rights reserved
including the right of reproduction
in whole or in part in any form.

John Niesel
Framing History
Fort Collins, Colorado

Email: info@FramingHistory.com
www.FramingHistory.com

First Edition: October 2008

ISBN 978-0-615-25633-7

Printed and bound in the United States of America.

*To Harold Brown –
A devoted father and grandfather,
a patriotic American,
and a friend.*

Contents

Acknowledgements *xiii*
Author's Note *xxiii*

Prologue *3*

ONE
This is the Army, Mr. Brown *6*

TWO
Birth of the Deuce *18*

THREE
Banana Boats and U-boats *24*

FOUR
Bogs, Rain, and Echoes of the Blitz *36*

FIVE
Utah Beach *56*

SIX
Danger in the Hedgerows, Grasshoppers in the Sky *66*

SEVEN
COBRA and Tigers *100*

EIGHT
Death in the Gap   *116*

NINE
Patton Races for Paris   *124*

TEN
Communication SNAFU's   *134*

ELEVEN
September 12, 1944   *144*

TWELVE
Mud, Snow...and the Bulge   *154*

THIRTEEN
NORDWIND   *184*

FOURTEEN
Winter in the Vosges Mountains   *198*

FIFTEEN
With the 3rd Infantry   *218*

SIXTEEN
Assaulting the Rhine   *236*

SEVENTEEN
Bread, Butter, and POW's   *262*

EIGHTEEN
Fall of Nuremberg...Death at Dachau   *282*

NINETEEN
Autobahn to Salzburg *310*

TWENTY
Raiding Hitler's Dining Room *328*

TWENTY-ONE
The Holy Right Hand *348*

TWENTY-TWO
Victory in Europe, Farewell to the Deuce *372*

TWENTY-THREE
Of Latrine Canvas & Cigarette Camps *380*

TWENTY-FOUR
Life After War *394*

TWENTY-FIVE
Return of the Crown *400*

Endnotes *415*

Bibliography *417*

Index *419*

Maps

The Cotentin Peninsula and D-Day Invasion Beaches	*62*
Utah Beach and Areas Inland	*79*
Operation COBRA	*102*
The Falaise Gap	*120*
Charmes, France, September 12, 1944	*146*
The American Front, late-December 1944	*181*
Operation NORDWIND	*196*
Guisberg, France, in the Vosges Mountains	*204*
Crossing the Rhine at Worms, Germany	*258*
Nuremberg, Germany, to Dachau, Germany	*309*
Munich, Germany to Salzburg, Austria	*321*
Berchtesgaden, Austria	*336*
Mattsee, Austria	*351*

Regarding Howitzers - Give me four days of clear weather so that my reconnaissance may pick out targets for my magnificent artillery.

> GENERAL GEORGE S. PATTON
> *Patton's Prayer*

Regarding Grasshoppers - We conducted extensive tests of the usefulness of the cub plane for observation purposes. These planes enabled our long-range artillery to gain an accuracy and quickness of adjustment previously restricted to the light guns within eyeshot of the target. Their worth was demonstrated conclusively.

> GENERAL DWIGHT D. EISENHOWER
> *Crusade in Europe*

Regarding The Holy Right Hand - It was a human hand, enclosed in a glass carrier, and it had all of these jewels around it...rubies and pearls and emeralds...
it was fascinating.

> HAROLD E. BROWN
> *Howitzers, Grasshoppers,*
> *and the Holy Right Hand*

Acknowledgements

Reading about events in history is one thing, but *seeing* the people, places and things is something else entirely. Harold Brown's story of his experiences in World War II is engaging in its own right, and I owe Harold my most sincere thanks for his patience, willingness, and openness during the many visits we spent recording, videotaping and talking about his memories. Those are hours I will cherish forever.

His recollections of the war were recorded not just in his mind, but in a small collection of curled, faded photographs that he had held on to for the past 60 years. Seeing faces of men he talked about, and of the places he had been, allowed me to better visualize the experience he was describing. As I stated above, his story is very engaging, but the addition of visual records enriches the reader's experience manyfold. It's one thing to say that the mud in eastern France during the wet fall of 1944 was almost deep enough to swallow a jeep...it's quite another thing to see a photograph of it.

As I set about writing this book, I began to believe that it would be made all the more "richer" if relevant photographs could be included. Harold's collection was a start, but it was very limited in scope. I needed a broader palette of photographs from which I could "paint" a visual picture for the reader. The obvious destinations for my search were the collections at the National Archives, as well as the thousands of photographs taken by the United States Army Signal Corps in World War II. But it was the not-so-obvious sources that have yielded the most relevant photographs of Harold's wartime experience. By luck and determination, I was fortunate to come across over 100 photographs that documented Harold's travels through France, Germany and Austria. By equal good fortune, the owners of these photographs were gracious enough to allow the use of the images in this book. For that kind gesture, I am extremely grateful to Rich Heller, Rod O'Barr, Dylan Thuras and Denis Toomey.

Rich has a web site dedicated to his dad, Sgt. Bill Heller. It may be viewed at www.warfoto.com.

Rod also has a web site dedicated to his dad, T/5 (Cpl) Milt O'Barr. It may be viewed by searching the following keywords: *85th Engineer Heavy Ponton Battalion*.

Dylan resides in Europe, and he provided the recent photographs of the "treasures" you will be reading about. His web site may be viewed at www.CuriousExpeditions.org.

Denis has a web site as well that is dedicated to his father, T/4 (Sgt) Bill Toomey. It may be viewed at www.dogfacesoldiers.org.

Of course, the GI's who took the photographs are the ones who made such a visual record possible, and I believe it is important to introduce them to the reader. Their photographs play an integral part in the telling of Harold's story, and their pictures are on the following pages, listed alphabetically by last name.

I must thank two people for providing the encouragement to undertake this project. My friend Jim Madewell, in response to a photo journal I completed in 2006, wrote, "I hope someday you will write a book" about World War II history. I think he planted a seed in my subconscious with that comment.

To my wife, Julie, I am wholly indebted. She not only encouraged me to see this book through to completion, but supported my belief that Harold's story was a story worth telling. When I doubted my capability to do justice to Harold's recollections, she was there to keep me focused. She offered constructive criticism throughout, and edited the finished draft of the manuscript, a task for which I cannot thank her enough. For many months she put up with my single-minded focus on the book, and she was the main sounding board for my thoughts and ideas. I could not have written Harold's story without her.

Photograph courtesy of Rich Heller   warfoto.com

Staff Sergeant William Heller of the 3rd Signal Company, 3rd Infantry Division, poses with his tools of the trade. Born and raised in Chicago, Bill volunteered for the U.S. Army at the age of 33. Even though his specialty was photography, the Army trained him as a rifleman, and Bill served in that capacity through the invasions of North Africa, Sicily, and Italy before being assigned to the Signal Corps in June 1944. Documenting the 3rd ID's France-Germany-Austria campaign on film through the end of the war, Bill was awarded the Bronze Star for his performance as a Combat Photographer.

Photograph courtesy of Milt L. O'Barr Collection

T/5 Milt L. O'Barr of the 85th Engineer Heavy Ponton Battalion. Milt, along with his twin brother, Mel, joined the United States Army in 1941. Over the next 4 ½ years, they found themselves carrying out their engineering duties in North Africa, Italy, France, Germany and Austria. Although it is unknown if Milt and Mel met Harold Brown and the 202nd Field Artillery Battalion, they nonetheless crossed paths at least twice during the campaign in Europe.

Photograph by Third Signal Company. Courtesy of dogfacesoldiers.org

T/4 William Toomey of Everett, Massachusetts, was drafted into the U.S. Army in 1943, and trained as a radio operator. He entered combat with the 15th Infantry Regiment during the near-calamitous amphibious invasion of Anzio in Italy. He was soon assigned to the Third Reconnaissance Battle Patrol, which assisted in the breakout from the Anzio beachhead and the drive to Rome. After the fall of the Eternal City, Bill was reassigned to the 3rd Signal Company due to his professional experience in newspaper photography. His efforts in photographing the 3rd Infantry Division's drive through France and into Germany were recognized with the awarding of a Bronze Star.

Photograph by Third Signal Company.   Courtesy of dogfacesoldiers.org

Pictured are four of the five photographers who comprised the 3rd Signal Company. From left:
John "Jack" Cole
William "Bill" Heller
William "Bill" Toomey
Robert "Bobby" Seesock

Not pictured is Howard Nickelson.

The amazing photographic record of the 3rd Infantry Division's march through Europe exists thanks to the courage and skill of these five men.

To Jim Barrett fell the task of proofreading the finished manuscript. The generous offer of his time and honest input is greatly appreciated. I owe you a Fat Tire (or two!). Any errors or omissions in the text are, of course, my own.

I used five main sources of reference during the writing of this book. Foremost among them were the video and oral interviews with Harold Brown that were conducted over an 18 month period.

The unit history of the 202nd Field Artillery Battalion provided me with dates, locations and actions involving the "Deuce".

The History of the 3rd Infantry Division in WW II, by Donald Taggart, provided me with the same for the Division.

The United States Army Center of Military History published two brochures that provided an overall summary of the actions in Europe in late-1944 through March 1945. These provided relevant information on the movements that Harold Brown was a part of. The brochures are:
Ardennes-Alsace: The U.S. Army Campaigns of World War II, by Roger Cirillo; *Rhineland: The U.S. Army Campaigns of World War II*, by Ted Ballard.

Using these references allowed me to verify the information provided by Harold Brown and the 202nd's unit history as these two sources form the factual backbone of the story. Through it all, Harold's penchant for accurately recalling dates, places and people was amazing. As Wayne, his son, told me, "When he's talking with you, he's a 26-year-old Captain on the battlefields of Europe again."

I employ endnotes extensively in two chapters, "Raiding Hitler's Dining Room" and "Return of the Crown", as the prior historical accounts discussed in both are a little, shall we say, contradictory, and open to debate. I suppose the fact that there are two or three differing versions of events may be attributed to the "fog of war". The differing accounts of the royal treasures may be nearly impossible to reconcile. Suffice it to say, however, that, regarding the Holy Right Hand, Harold Brown's account offers the most detailed explanation yet. His experience is, I believe, the most accurate, and I am convinced it is true. Harold has nothing to gain by making his claims; the same cannot be said by others who had much to gain at the end of the war. It is important for the correct history to be told.

I don't know if this book will shed some light on what really occurred in Berchtesgaden or with the relics; at the very least it may fill in some of the missing details.

I leave it to the reader to decide.

Author's Note

On the morning of December 15, 2005, I was at work in my framing shop when my phone rang.

I answered, "Thanks for calling Framing History. This is John, may I help you?"

"Yes, my name is Harold Brown," the voice on the other end said. "I saw that you make frames for veterans, and I have some items I would like to have framed."

"I'd be more than happy to help," I said. "What is it you would like framed?"

Harold replied, "Oh, just a couple of medals and some papers."

Before the call ended we arranged a time to meet. The next day I paid a visit to he and his wife, and I learned about Harold Brown's "Just a couple of medals and some papers…"

Unexpectedly, however, I also heard the beginning of an intriguing story about a brave, young American from the tiny farming community of Johnstown, Colorado, who joined 16 million of his countrymen and women on a crusade to free the world from tyranny and oppression.

Of course I was very enthused to assist Harold in commemorating a part of his personal history; I had no idea that two years later I would be writing about it.

As Harold and I visited over those two years, he shared with me more and more of his experiences as a young officer in the U.S. Army; experiences which spanned the time from when he enlisted prior to the attack on Pearl Harbor to the day of his mustering-out after VJ Day.

World War II had lasted six long, grim and bloody years, and during that dark time in the world's history, Harold went from the family farm in Johnstown to the beaches of Normandy, across France into central Germany, then south to Austria and the city of Salzburg. He actively participated in many of the major actions that were fought in those areas of Europe, experiencing many of the horrors and the waste of war along the way.

His duty in Europe concluded, though, with his participation in the recovery of a most unusual, highly-revered religious icon, along with unique treasures that were "fit for a king."

As I researched dates, places and event timelines, the accuracy of Harold's recollections struck me as remarkable, for more than 60 years had passed since the events had occurred. He was in the Regular Army for over 4 ½ years during the War, a time during which he was both an observer and a participant in history; a time when he experienced many, many things, both ordinary and extraordinary. Obviously he doesn't recall all that he did and saw, but certain events and experiences are burned into his memory.

Consequently, this book is not meant to be a detailed, day-by-day accounting of Harold's time in the service, nor a complete recounting of the War. Rather, it may be viewed as a collection of interrelated events as recalled by Harold; perhaps it's best to look upon it as a narrative journal of sorts.

Harold's contribution to the victory over fascism in World War II was important to him...
...and after hearing it personally, I realized his contribution had to be shared with others.

This is the story of Captain Harold E. Brown, United States Army Artillery, World War II, and I am truly honored to share his experiences with you.

John Niesel
November 2007

Howitzers
Grasshoppers
and the Holy Right Hand

★ ★ ★ ★ ★ ★ ★ ★

The Wartime Experiences Of
Captain Harold E. Brown
United States Army Artillery
World War II

Prologue

★ ★ ★

"Brown, take care of that".

With those few words that were spoken in the waning days of World War II in Europe, a series of events were set in motion that would impact not just Captain Harold Brown and his men, but also the population of a war-torn nation. The complete legacy of Harold Brown's actions would not be fully realized until over 30 years later, long-delayed due to another conflict, the Cold War.

In May of 1945, however, with the end of the war in Europe rapidly approaching, Captain Harold Brown, 202nd Field Artillery Battalion, United States Army, had only immediate tasks on his mind.

It had been a long ten months since he landed on French soil at Utah Beach in July of 1944, just 3 ½ weeks after the initial D-Day landings. Since coming ashore, the 155mm howitzers of the "Deuce-O-Deuce" had been in action nearly non-stop, from the Normandy hedgerow country outside of Carentan, to the deadly Falaise Pocket, then the race across France to the German border. They crossed the mighty Rhine River, moved swiftly into Bavaria, and sped down Adolf Hitler's autobahn to Salzburg, Austria. The Third Reich was crumbling rapidly, the soldiers of the Wehrmacht surrendering by the thousands.

The war news wasn't all good, however. Each day brought new revelations of unspeakable Nazi atrocities against humanity, and there were rumors of fanatical SS troops assembling in the nearby mountains of southern Germany, tasked by their now-dead Führer to wage a guerilla war against the Allies.

There were also unusual discoveries and happenings in those final days of the conflict, stories and news reports of Allied troops uncovering hidden stashes of stolen artwork and treasure, brought to Germany and Austria by the Wehrmacht and Luftwaffe during their nearly unchecked march through Europe in 1939 and 1940.

Consequently, when Captain Brown queried his commanding officer, Lieutenant Colonel Tom Lewis, what exactly he was supposed to "take care of", Lieutenant Colonel Lewis told him, "The OSS has some treasure up there and wants some backup". "Up there" was the little town of Mattsee, Austria, 14 miles northeast of Salzburg,

PROLOGUE

close to the German border. There were no further details, and it was a mystery as to exactly what the treasure was.

Therefore, without any other information regarding what to expect in the way of enemy resistance, Harold Brown assembled a squad of riflemen, requisitioned two trucks that were outfitted with mounted .50 caliber heavy machine guns, and prepared to set off on his mission.

Little did he know what he was about to find.

Harold Brown Collection

2ⁿᵈ Lieutenant Harold E. Brown
Photographed after receiving his commission
as an officer in the United States Army.
June 1941

Chapter 1

This is the Army, Mr. Brown

★ ★ ★ ★ ★ ★ ★ ★ ★

Johnstown is a small farming community located on the high plains of north-central Colorado. While growing up there on the family farm, Harold Brown would often look to the west where, beyond the vast fields of sugar beets, oats and barley, he could see the sweeping vista of the Front Range of the Rocky Mountains.

As Harold looked out of the shattered picture window in the bombed-out Berghof in the spring of 1945, the mountain views before him were vivid reminders of the familiar Colorado mountain scenery, and of home.

★ ★ ★

Four years prior to 1945, Harold was attending Colorado State College of Agriculture and Mechanic Arts in

Fort Collins, 30 miles northwest of Johnstown, where he was nearing the completion of his studies for a degree in Agronomy.

Due to A&M's status as a land grant institution, all able-bodied males enrolled at the college were required to take part in some military training.

"The first two years were required, and the second two years were optional," Harold explains. "If you wanted to be considered for an officer's commission, you had to finish the extra two years of ROTC advanced training, which happened to pay $250."

No small sum in 1939, the money was an important factor in Harold's decision. "I took the $250," he says with a smile.

On May 26, 1941, the day that he received his college diploma, Harold also received his commission as a 2nd Lieutenant in the United States Army Artillery. As he would be quickly receiving orders to report for active duty, Harold had very little time for celebrating his graduation. Therefore, with his diploma and commission in hand, he bid farewell to Fort Collins and Colorado A&M, and returned to the family farm for what was destined to be a very short stay.

Though America was officially uninvolved in the conflicts that were overtaking Europe and Asia in the spring of 1941, the rumblings of war nevertheless reverberated across the nation, and the ill-prepared branches of the

United States military were scrambling to rectify their numerous shortcomings. As a result, the U.S. Armed Forces were training men by the thousands, and on May 31, 1941, Uncle Sam came calling for Harold.

Consequently, a brief ten days later, 2nd Lieutenant Harold Brown was at Fort Sill, Oklahoma, attending Artillery School.

★   ★   ★

Though war raged in Europe and the Far East in mid-1941, Harold Brown and the men training with him did not give too much thought to the war clouds that were growing ever more ominous.

"I think the higher-ups in Washington knew it was coming, but we didn't know for sure," Harold states. "Actually, we really didn't think about it much at all. We were too busy studying!"

For Harold and his classmates, training was serious business. The artillery students were issued numerous Army Field Manuals, the contents of which each student was thoroughly tested on.

According to Harold, the dedicated studying time the manuals required was as much as, if not more than, what was required for college coursework. In fact there was *so* much to read, that, in order to be able to catch some sleep at night, Harold had to skim the paragraph headings, skipping those that he knew enough about, and devoting reading time to only the paragraphs he had no knowledge of.

"If I didn't," he says, "I would have been reading the assigned book from the time the class ended up, until we had the class the next day, and I *still* wouldn't have been able to finish all of the reading."

As a result of the intensive studying, the time passed quickly at Fort Sill. By mid-August 1941 Harold was beginning his third month of instruction at Artillery School. Graduation was only a few weeks away, but his training suffered a setback when tragedy unexpectedly struck his family.

"In August of '41 my Dad was killed in a farming accident," he relates. "The Army gave me a short leave so I could go home and help my mother with all that needed done. Not only did the funeral need to be arranged, but it was nearly harvest time, and our farm fields were full of crops."

Neighbor helping neighbor was a hallmark of rural Colorado life in the 1930's and 1940's, and fortunately, neighbors of the Brown's graciously offered to help with the fall harvest. This kind, selfless act was indeed a great relief to the grieving family, and Harold and his two younger brothers were therefore able to focus their attention on their mother, and on helping her with the many necessary arrangements that needed taken care of.

★ ★ ★

Harold's dad, Robert Brown, was laid to rest, and shortly after the funeral Harold headed back to Oklahoma knowing that he had done all he could for his mother in the short leave time he was allotted.

Upon his return to Fort Sill, Harold was informed that he had missed a great deal of coursework; his instructors felt he couldn't possibly catch up with his classmates before graduation. Therefore, he was placed back two classes, slated to repeat a majority of the instruction he had already received.

Undeterred, Harold continued on with his schooling, which meant many more nights devoted to studying the ubiquitous Army Field Manuals. In spite of his disappointment, over the next 60 days he nonetheless became well-schooled in the operation and tactics of the Field Artillery.

Harold completed the final tests with relative ease, and upon graduation from Artillery School he received his first assignment; he was soon on his way to the United States Army's 2nd Infantry Division, 12th Field Artillery Regiment at Fort Sam Houston, Texas.

★ ★ ★

HOWITZERS, GRASSHOPPERS, AND THE HOLY RIGHT HAND

As at military bases across the U.S. in 1941, Fort Sam Houston had thousands of draftees and enlistees arriving in a steady stream, and all of these new GI's required instruction in the methods and skills that would make them an effective part of the rapidly expanding American military force.

With Hitler's Nazis in control of Western Europe and with Imperial Japan pursuing expansionist policies in the Pacific Ocean and Asia, the United States military high command realized that time was of the essence. Consequently, training of the new GI's was a continuous process with group after group of men arriving for indoctrination into the ways and routines of the U.S. Army.

In early December 1941, Harold traveled from Fort Sam Houston back to Fort Sill where he escorted a group of soldiers for additional training.

As the construction of barracks had not caught up with demand, the officers and enlisted men slept in canvas tents, shelters which did not provide much insulation from the cold Oklahoma nights. Adding to their discomfort were the many hours each day they spent training on the wintry, windswept plains. Consequently, with Christmas only a few weeks away, many of the men were looking forward to the upcoming holiday leave which would bring them not only warmth, but a welcome respite from Army routine as well.

Imperial Japan, however, had far different plans for the men of the United States military.

On December 7, 1941, Harold and his artillerymen's thoughts of home dissipated as quickly as their frosty breath did in the dry, Oklahoma winter air.

"We got the word of what had happened at Pearl Harbor," Harold remembers, "and orders right behind that were, 'Pack up all of your civilian clothes and send them home.' So that's what we did."

Lieutenant Brown and his fellow soldiers would not be in need of their "civvies" any time soon. They quickly gathered up their gear and headed back to Fort Sam Houston; unbeknownst to Harold, his stay there was destined to be short.

The U.S. Armed Forces were undergoing major growth and reorganization throughout 1941, and the outbreak of war led to an even greater sense of urgency. Officers and men were being shifted around to form new divisions and battalions, and Lieutenant Harold Brown was one of those in the shuffle.

"The colonel came in and told me that the 45th Division put out a call for some young officers," he remembers, "and as I was one of the last to join the 12th Field Artillery Regiment, I was going to be one of the first to be reassigned."

Therefore, as the New Year approached, Harold found himself on his way to the 2nd Battalion of the 189th Field Artillery Regiment, which was attached to the 45th Infantry

HOWITZERS, GRASSHOPPERS, AND THE HOLY RIGHT HAND

Division at Camp Barkeley, Texas. This time he hoped he could stay with the same battalion for a while.

As things turned out, he would be with them for the next 3 ½ years.

☆   ☆   ☆

In the immediate days after December 7th, 1941, the United States was working frantically to get not only the Armed Forces on a wartime footing, but the American population and U.S. industrial might as well. The immense, unprecedented challenges faced by the Nation's woefully unprepared military, public and private sectors were multiplied many-fold when, on December 11, 1941, Adolf Hitler went before his Nazi minions at the Reichstag in Berlin and declared that a state of war now existed between Germany and the United States.

Almost overnight, America found herself facing a world-wide war on two fronts, and Hitler's declaration left many servicemen wondering in what part of the world they would eventually find themselves fighting.

Like most soldiers in the U.S. Army, Harold had no idea where he would ultimately be deployed, and he says he really didn't think about it much. His concentration was focused instead on the job at hand, for there was plenty at hand to do.

"In early 1942 I was promoted to 1st Lieutenant and given command of one of the three batteries that comprised the battalion," he recalls. "Our weapon was the 155mm howitzer, and each battery had four howitzers."

Unlike the long-barreled field guns that fired a shell on a relatively flat trajectory over longer distances, the short-barreled howitzer could fire its shell on a high trajectory. This arc allowed the howitzer round to hit targets that were not reachable by the long-barreled field guns, targets such as those that would be found on the backside of a hill. Whereas a flatter-trajectory shell would hit the front of the hill or pass over it completely, the howitzer round would be "lobbed" over the hilltop, coming down at a high angle to hit the targets that were dug in on the reverse slope.

The 155mm Howitzer M1 employed by the 189th Field Artillery Regiment was a very effective weapon when used correctly, and Harold's job was to make sure his men would employ the guns as such.

"As a battery commander I had 125 men under me," explains Harold. "I trained them extensively over the following months with a combination of classroom instruction, participation in field maneuvers and firing range practice."

A ten-man gun crew was assigned to a howitzer, and each crew was responsible for their artillery piece. Just as an infantryman has his personal rifle, and a pilot his assigned aircraft, the artillery crews had their own howitzer, and therefore knew their weapon inside and out.

Ultimately though, responsibility for the performance of the battery fell on Harold's shoulders, and he worked hard to prepare the men for the tasks they would be called upon to perform.

Utilizing a continuing training regimen, Lieutenant Brown did his best to ensure that his gun crews and support sections worked hard to become a well-oiled team. With their combined efforts, Harold was confident that his men would be fully capable of deploying their weapons quickly, and able to deliver accurate fire as a dependable, vital component of the 189th Field Artillery Regiment.

Harold Brown Collection

Lieutenant Harold Brown, photographed by a street photographer in Beaumont, Texas, in 1942. Harold decided to support the "artist" by purchasing a copy of the photograph.

Chapter 2

Birth of the Deuce

★ ★ ★ ★ ★ ★ ★ ★

As part of the reorganization undertaken by the United States Army during 1941 and 1942, old-line "square" divisions composed of four infantry regiments were being converted to "triangle" divisions of three infantry regiments.

Simply put, in the United States Army, an "Army Group" was comprised of "Armies", an "Army" (like Patton's Third Army) was comprised of "Corps"; a "Corps" was comprised of "Divisions"; a "Division" was comprised of "Regiments"; a "Regiment" was comprised of "Battalions".

The "Thunderbirds" of the 45th Infantry Division went through the conversion process, and as a result, the 1st Battalion of the 189th Field Artillery Regiment became a stand-alone artillery battalion, assigned to provide fire support at the Corps level.

Hence the 202nd Field Artillery Battalion, the "Deuce-O-Deuce" came into existence.

The transition was relatively easy as the entire 1st Battalion rolled-over to the Deuce. Men who had trained together as early as Sept. 16, 1940, would remain together, and would continue training as a cohesive unit.

Although they were not aware of it during the frantic and confusing initial months of the war, this training would be ongoing for the next 2 ½ years.

☆ ☆ ☆

During this time in early 1942, Harold Brown received a promotion to Captain, and consequently was moved up to Battalion Staff. His own training now included becoming proficient with the responsibilities of the Battalion S-2, Intelligence Officer.

In this position, it fell upon Harold to scout out routes and locations ahead of the unit when the battalion was ordered to redeploy, and further obligated him to learn the skills of a forward observer. This required him to observe, register and correct the Deuce's artillery fire, which he did from positions on the ground, as well as in the sky from Piper Cub L-4 observation planes.

These small, slow, fabric-covered aircraft, which were nicknamed "Grasshoppers" due to their ability to operate from small, grassy strips and fields, allowed the U.S. Army's artillery observers to quickly direct accurate shell fire on a designated target.

The aerial spotting abilities that Harold developed during training and maneuvers in 1942 and 1943 were valuable skills that he came to greatly appreciate in the days ahead.

"I used that training as much as anything once I was in combat," he states. "As soon as I saw where the first round fell, we could accurately correct the fire so the next salvo would hit on or near the target. Everyone gained proficiency with repetition, and we practiced and practiced over and over."

Operation of the howitzers had to become second nature for the men; the repetitive training was carried out with the knowledge that the payoff in efficiency would benefit the Battalion once the Deuce was engaged in combat. When that time came, the GI's of the 202nd Field Artillery Battalion knew that accuracy and quickness on their part could quite possibly mean the difference between life and death.

Throughout all of 1942 and into 1943 the Deuce's training continued, whether in the heat and humidity of southern summers or in the bitter, winter cold of the wind-blown American plains. These months of preparation would see them traveling back and forth across the southern

Harold Brown Collection

24 year-old Captain Harold Brown at Camp Gruber, Oklahoma, 1942.

United States, participating in maneuvers throughout Louisiana, Oklahoma and Texas, and eventually overseas...but just where overseas, they still did not know.

The time was rapidly approaching, however, when they would finally find out: the beginning of February in the new year of 1944 would see the Deuce's howitzers bellowing their loud report over the peat bogs of Ireland, and the grassy green fields of Wales.

U.S. Army Signal Corps

United States Army personnel en route to Ireland. The 10 day Atlantic voyage on cramped, crowded ships was usually marked by hours upon hours of boredom. GI's often congregated on deck to breathe some fresh air, and to shoot the breeze with their comrades. Note the lifebelts around the waists of the soldiers, a requirement when onboard ship.

Chapter 3

Banana Boats and U-boats

☆ ☆ ☆ ☆ ☆ ☆ ☆ ☆

On Christmas Day 1943, the Deuce received a long-awaited gift from the Army command: they were alerted to prepare for overseas shipment.

The men of the 202nd Field Artillery Battalion began the arduous task of readying their equipment, their personal items and themselves for the ocean voyage, a complicated process which required ten days. Everything had to be packed carefully in order to ensure survival from damage during the long transit, and all items had to be labeled accurately to ensure arrival at the proper destination if they survived undamaged.

The men did their best, and crossed their fingers that their efforts would not be in vain.

HOWITZERS, GRASSHOPPERS, AND THE HOLY RIGHT HAND

Once the preparations were complete, the equipment was shipped out via freight train, and the men boarded passenger coaches for the long rail ride to the Atlantic coast. However, due to the congestion that afflicted the country's overloaded railroads throughout the war, the 202nd FA Bn's train was assigned a less-than-direct route.

"They sent another battalion and us at the same time," Harold recalls, "but the other battalion was routed east through Texas and then up the East Coast, a pretty direct route to the ports of embarkation." No such luck for the men of the Deuce.

From Camp Howes in Texas, Harold and the men traveled north into the Midwest, then the upper-Midwest. Next it was on into Canada, then east to the Atlantic coast...not exactly the quickest path to their destination, which was Camp Miles Standish in Taunton, Massachusetts, just outside of Boston. But at the time, it was the only route available.

★ ★ ★

While en route to the camp, most of the men of the Deuce had time to relax and reflect on what the future had in store for them. As it turned out for Harold, though, he would find himself with very little time for relaxation and contemplation. He was too busy learning another skill.

"Well, I was appointed Mess Officer for the train." Then he adds wryly, "...with no training for being the Mess Officer."

To this day he still doesn't know why he was chosen, but prefers to believe it was due to his commanding officer's trust in him. Harold would do the job properly and well, but it did have its challenges. For example, it was impossible to serve so many men at the few tables available on board the train.

"We fed the troops in their seats," he explains. 'We had these big kettles, and the guys would lug them down the aisles. The men all had their mess kits out. We would scoop out a bunch of stew and dump it into their mess kits. Not exactly the fanciest way to eat, but it worked."

Cooking meals for 500 GI's was a time-consuming event that required careful coordination and orchestration, a task that was made all the more difficult by the constraints imposed by the railroad's kitchen car.

"We didn't have time to cook three meals a day," Harold states, "so the men were fed two times a day. However we did have some station stops where waiting for us on the platforms were women who had goodies to pass out...donuts, coffee and the like from the Servicemen's Canteens."

Harold never got to partake of any of these treats, however. He spent his station stops overseeing the loading of foodstuffs onto the train.

HOWITZERS, GRASSHOPPERS, AND THE HOLY RIGHT HAND

"As Mess Officer I had to buy for the menus ahead of time" he says. "I had never done this before. Luckily, I had with me Lieutenant Samuel Giannetto who had worked as a Mess Officer somewhere. He was a tailor by trade, from New York I believe, and he helped me set up the menus, which was not an easy job because we were allowed to spend only 70 cents a day, per man, for food."

Consequently, figuring out just the right amount of food to buy was no easy task. A task which, if not done correctly, would result in either angry, underfed GI's, or a meal budget that was exceeded. The former may get you dirty looks and negative comments, but the latter could hit you where it hurts...in the wallet.

Harold relates, "South of Chicago we decided we needed lettuce, carrots...some greenery for the men. We wired on ahead to a supplier to meet us at the train with our order, which was quite a bit; I think it came in two trucks. We unloaded the lettuce and other vegetables, so the men could have a salad. We also bought many sides of beef, trying to calculate everything as close as we could."

Harold worried that he was going to exceed his mess budget, because as Mess Officer, he would personally have to pay the Army for any amount spent over the budgeted 70 cents a day per man. Fortunately, as things turned out, Harold's wallet was safe.

"When I got to Massachusetts, I was the only mess officer there who had money to turn in," he says, smiling. "There were a lot of guys standing there who had brought in troops, and all of them had over-spent their budget, and they were responsible for repaying it."

Harold was relieved to have fed the men well, and to have come in under budget. However, he gives credit where credit is due.

"Giannetto did a good job at figuring out the menus," he says. "I was a rookie."

A rookie, maybe. But he was a rookie who did such a good job that his commanding officer decided to "honor" Harold with the same assignment again. This time, for the long voyage over the Atlantic.

★   ★   ★

The men of the 202nd Field Artillery Battalion arrived at Camp Miles Standish on January 11, 1944.

As a major port of embarkation on the East Coast, the camp was a beehive of activity with all of the preparations for the upcoming invasion of Europe. Men and equipment were being shipped to the United Kingdom in a never-ending stream, and on January 19th, it was the Deuce's turn to join the parade of convoys headed east.

With the huge requirements placed on the naval and merchant ships at that time, vessels of all types were pressed into service as freighters and troop transports.

Some men traveled on converted luxury liners, some on Navy troopships.

The GI's of the Deuce drew a Cuban banana boat.

"I believe that was its last voyage," says Harold. "I think they just trashed it after we got off!"

For Harold, the trip overseas was similar to voyages experienced by many Americans headed to the European Theater of Operations (ETO): crowded conditions onboard ship, overflowing buckets of vomit from seasick GI's, U-boat scares, and the nasty North Atlantic weather.

"It was a pretty big boat, but it was jam-packed with over a thousand men on board," Harold recalls. "There were two artillery battalions and a Graves Registration company stuffed in the ship. The crew didn't know where to put all of us."

Sleeping quarters for all of the men were makeshift at best. The banana holds of the old ship were now filled with stacked bunks hanging from chains, beds which swung too and fro with the rolling motion of the ship as it plowed through the North Atlantic swells.

For those men who couldn't, or didn't want to, bunk in the hot, cigarette smoke-filled hold below, other arrangements were made with beds placed up on the deck of the ship. At least the air was fresher there.

Unfortunately, the cramped living conditions weren't the worst part.

U.S. Army Signal Corps

The monotony of the ocean crossing was occasionally interrupted by lifeboat drill. A few of the men in the photograph are wearing kapok lifejackets in lieu of the more-common lifebelt. If worn too low on the body of a combat-loaded GI, the lifebelt had a tendency to float the wearer upside down, leading to many needless drownings.

HOWITZERS, GRASSHOPPERS, AND THE HOLY RIGHT HAND

"The trip over was rough," Harold remembers. "We were tossed around like a button on a string. Hundreds of the men were seasick. We were in some pretty high water on the North Atlantic. We got up where the waves were higher than the boat! Here you would look up on both sides of your boat, and all you could see were walls of water. If you stayed out on the deck, some of that would come crashing down on you."

Luckily, no one was swept overboard by the high waves, and the plodding convoy of ships continued on course, slowly making its way east through the perils of the sea.

★ ★ ★

The North Atlantic was infamous for its towering waves and rough waters. To minimize the hazards, the Deuce's pack of ships was supposed to stay to the south as long as possible. A new threat arose, however, which required a change in the convoy's planned course.

"We took a little detour on the way to Ireland," Harold explains. "We had an escort of DE's (Destroyer Escorts), and we got orders to turn and go north until further orders. It seems they had picked up a group of German submarines on our planned course."

German U-boats had been hunting prey in the waters of the Atlantic ever since the outbreak of war. Thousands of Allied ships had been torpedoed and sent to the bottom during that time, but the German "Untersee Boot" fleet had suffered heavy losses as well.

Enemy submarines still prowled the convoy routes, nevertheless, and evasive action was undertaken whenever there was a threat of a U-boat attack. Fortunately for the Deuce, the convoy avoided the German subs.

"The Navy tried to get us up and around the U-boats," Harold relates, "which they did. The Germans didn't give us any trouble."

When asked if he worried about being torpedoed, Harold's reply is pretty matter-of-fact.

"No, I didn't worry about it. I was in the game to do the best that I could do, no matter what happened."

☆   ☆   ☆

Despite high seas and U-boat scares, the GI's onboard the ship had to eat. Consequently, Harold went about his mess duties (he was one of the fortunate few who didn't get seasick), keeping busy overseeing the feeding of the 1150 men.

"The food we served wasn't too bad," he recalls. "It was just such a hassle trying to get everybody fed all of the time. We had to break them down into two meals a day, and all day we had a continuous line going through the mess hall. Some guys would finish one meal, then go back to the end of the queue to get in line for the next meal. My job was to keep the lines organized, and to check on the kitchen to see how they were doing."

Did he enjoy being Mess Officer?

"Not much...no," he says. "But they wanted me to do it, so I did it."

★ ★ ★

One stormy day led to another, and the daily routine onboard the ship continued without interruption across the wide expanse of the Atlantic Ocean.

Finally, ten long days after leaving the United States, Harold and the men of the Deuce set thankful eyes, and even more-thankful stomachs, upon the welcome shores of Ireland.

Harold Brown Collection

Captain Harold Brown (2nd from left) photographed during the months of training leading up to the Deuce's deployment to France.

Chapter 4

Bogs, Rain, and Echoes of the Blitz

★ ★ ★ ★ ★ ★ ★ ★

January 28, 1944, found the men of the 202nd Field Artillery Battalion safely on the docks in Belfast, Ireland.

Thankful to leave the banana boat and the tossing seas of the North Atlantic behind, Harold and his fellow artillerymen loaded into a convoy of trucks, which in turn transported them to the railway station where a train awaited. Once all were on board, the train pulled out of the station, and headed southwest.

It was a short trip. After just a few hours, the men arrived at their destination: Camp Drumilly, in County Armagh, 30 miles from Belfast.

★ ★ ★

Harold had a realistic view of their first overseas home.

"We set up in a bunch of Quonset huts," he recalls. "Everybody had a roof over their head, which was good because it rained a lot."

Yet despite the frequently wet weather, the Irish landscape struck a chord with him. "In Ireland everything was green," he says. "It was pretty country." However, nice as they were, the pleasant views would not compensate for being wet all of the time. Fortunately, the Quonsets were a big improvement over canvas tents, and the huts provided sturdy, dry shelter that was much appreciated.

★   ★   ★

The Deuce had left their howitzers and heavy equipment behind in the States; there it would be passed on to another artillery battalion. To replace it, vast stores of American war material populated fields and meadows throughout the U.K., and the Deuce drew new equipment from the nearest artillery supply depot.

With their shiny, new howitzers, trucks and jeeps, the 202nd Field Artillery Battalion embarked on three months of intensive training. A long series of field exercises commenced as soon as the new equipment was ready for use, and in rain or shine (and it was mostly rain), the battalion drilled over and over again.

U.S. Army Signal Corps

Quonset huts under construction at a U.S. Army camp in Ireland. These simple but sturdy structures provided warm and dry quarters for Harold Brown and his fellow artillerymen.

HOWITZERS, GRASSHOPPERS, AND THE HOLY RIGHT HAND

When the batteries were scheduled for firing practice, the battalion traveled north to the artillery range in the Sperrin Mountains. There they encountered some most unusual terrain.

"There were these peat bogs in the mountains of northern Ireland," Harold remembers. "Everything would sink down into the stuff: weapons, tractors, jeeps. The spongy peat would just swallow things up. It made for really difficult training."

"We did our best dealing with it, though. We practiced our firing and worked on our weapons to prepare for what we knew was coming soon."

The men of the Deuce recognized that eventually when they went into combat it wouldn't necessarily be under sunny skies and on dry, firm terrain.

★ ★ ★

Amidst all of the training and preparations for going to war, Harold recalls that there was still a little time for the men to participate in a few of the pursuits that always seemed popular with the American GI. Gambling, naturally, was high on the list of distractions, as well as searching out nearby pubs and taverns for a pint of ale.

"Some of the men lived for payday and the falderal that immediately followed," says Harold. "It's all they thought about."

BOGS, RAIN, AND ECHOES OF THE BLITZ

Not one for cards or craps, Harold left the games of chance to others. And in regards to pubs and taverns, being an officer meant he had to mind appearances, at least in public. Consequently, he remained on his best behavior.

Fraternizing with the local Irish townsfolk was yet another popular diversion, and attending a community dance increased ones chances of making the acquaintance of a local girl. It seems a little female companionship went a long way towards making a GI's day-to-day life more bearable. However, if you didn't gamble, drink or chase women, there was always food to think about, and Harold wasn't one to pass up a chance to supplement his GI grub!

"We'd sneak off across the peat fields to this house up the hill," he relates with a smile, "and we'd hire the woman who lived there to cook us steak and eggs! Just how many times we did it, I don't remember...but I always was game to do it!"

After all, an army does indeed fight on its stomach!

★   ★   ★

Gambling, drinking, fraternizing and searching for tasty non-GI food provided welcome distractions, and the days at Camp Drumilly went by quickly for Harold and the men. They realized, however, that they wouldn't remain in Ireland very long; the "big show" was due to start anytime.

When asked if he and his men knew that the Channel invasion was quickly approaching, Harold says they could tell it was. This feeling, however, did not impart a sense of additional urgency on him or his men.

"It was business as usual," he says. "We were already well trained to move the battalion and to fire our shells. It wasn't any big deal."

No doubt such confidence helped the men of the Deuce deal with their inner thoughts of what lay ahead, for the time of their entrance into combat was indeed coming soon.

★   ★   ★

All throughout the war, London, England, was a favored destination for America's GI's. Far from home and in search of entertainment, many of the "Yanks" traveled there on their weekend passes. Some men were eager to explore the city and its historic sights, while others just wanted to quaff a pint at one of the many pubs.

If sightseeing and warm beer didn't float one's boat, the streets of London offered a variety of diverse attractions and distractions to assist the young GI's in disposing of their monthly pay.

Harold, too, had an opportunity to visit England's capital, but his purpose was purely business.

In early February 1944, the Deuce's CO, Lieutenant Colonel Tom Lewis, decided to send Captain Brown to attend the Order of Battle School in downtown London. The classes taught at the school were designed to prepare Allied officers for German tactics that might be encountered in combat once the Allies invaded France. Harold's position as the Battalion Intelligence Officer meant that he would gain the most useful knowledge from the classes, which is why he was chosen to attend.

Looking forward to a change in routine, Harold hopped a train to England's capital city, and after checking in to a small hotel, he went to attend the classes which were being held nearby.

Harold has fond memories of the instructor, a Major Brawley of the British Infantry.

"He was a lively guy, very animated," Harold remembers, "and I thought he looked a lot like Sherlock Holmes!"

"He taught us how the German Army and divisions were organized, through their various levels. But what I found most interesting was the rundown they gave us on all of the personalities that we might run in to."

"For instance, we talked about Rommel. We were told that if we run up against him, this is the type of soldier he is. This is how he will react."

"We also discussed von Runstedt, and Sepp Dietrich, and several others. They gave us a review on all of them, and the kind of tactics you might encounter if you found yourself opposite them."

Harold found the information distributed in the class to be very helpful.

"They sent me so I would have an idea of what we might be confronted with when we got into combat," he explains. "And if we ran up against Rommel, which we did, we'd know a little bit about him."

* * *

The days spent at the Order of Battle School were the only time Harold found himself in London during the war. A dramatic change from rural Ireland, the bustling city streets were teeming with servicemen and women of many nationalities, while Londoners did their best to get on with their daily lives as normally as possible.

Though the Blitz had been over for years, just by chance the Luftwaffe decided to pay London a visit one night while Harold was there.

"I was staying in what was known as the Audley Hotel," he begins, "and the air raid whistles and bells started to ring."

"Everybody was supposed to go down to the air raid shelters in the subway, but I stayed and stood in my window and watched the sky as the planes came in. They were dropping foil of some kind to mess up the radar signals."

Not exactly in the safest place, Harold nonetheless stayed at his window, too transfixed by the German bombers to head for the air raid shelter.

"Then the bombs came down," he relates. "The Germans just seemed to be dropping them at random, like they didn't have any specific target," an actuality he realized as soon as the bombs starting exploding nearby.

"Some of them hit real close to the hotel," he says, "and the buildings crumbled over into the street. The British searchlights were sweeping the sky, the anti-aircraft guns were firing. I don't know if any planes were shot down, but I got to see some of it anyway. Eventually it quieted down and I went to bed."

When he woke up in the morning and looked out of his window, Harold viewed a prime example of the now-famous determination and fortitude exhibited by the British people during World War II. With a tone of amazement in his voice even today, Harold describes the scene.

"When I got up, *all* of the bricks that had fallen into the street had been picked up and stacked in neat little rows alongside the street, and the street was already open," he recalls. "The British had a *real* good system for cleaning up the mess after a bombing."

When asked if standing at a London hotel window wasn't such a smart thing to do during a Luftwaffe air raid, Harold admits, "Well yeah, it was getting kind of scary, and I got to thinking that maybe I should have followed the rules and gone down to the subway. But it was too late so I just watched it out."

Harold was lucky that night, and he hoped his luck would continue to carry him through the trying days that he knew were ahead of him.

★   ★   ★

As the day for the invasion of France crept closer, so too the men of the Deuce moved nearer to the location of their departure, the southeast coast of England.

In early May 1944 the battalion left Ireland, sailing from Belfast, past the Isle of Man, to the port of Liverpool. Then it was southeast 120 miles to Wheatley, a small English town just east of Oxford.

The Deuce's new home wasn't at all like the established camp they had left behind in Ireland.

"We were quartered in an alfalfa field along with another Field Artillery Battalion, the 961st," Harold describes. "Unlike the barracks we had in Ireland, here everybody had tents. We set up our pup tents and organized it so the batteries would all be together."

It had the look of a temporary camp, which indeed it was, and gave them a small foretaste of the living conditions they would encounter in Europe. As events would play out, it would be quite a while before the men of the Deuce slept with a solid roof over their heads.

As in the U.S and Ireland, live-fire training continued while the Deuce was based at Wheatley. In order to conduct such firing practice, the 155's were transported to firing ranges in Wales, including a visit to the primary British artillery range in the Sennybridge Mountains. The battalion was there, taking part in a routine firing problem on the day of June 6, 1944.

"We were in Wales when the message came that the invasion was starting," Harold remembers. "So we packed up right away and went back to Wheatley. We started to get the Battalion organized so we would be ready to go when ordered."

It was during this time of final pre-combat preparation that the Battalion's equipment was waterproofed for the Channel crossing, and also when the Deuce drew its last batch of new heavy equipment.

"We were using trucks, Diamond T's we called them, to pull the howitzers," Harold says. "A couple of weeks before we left for Normandy we were issued new prime movers, which were tractors with treads. They could traverse rough ground better than the Diamond T's."

The men of the 202nd Field Artillery Battalion underwent intensive training on the maintenance and operation of the new M-5 "cats". Though they knew all of

Photograph courtesy of Rich Heller   warfoto.com

An M-5 Tractor towing a howitzer. The Deuce received these "cats" as replacements for the prime mover trucks they had previously used.

their older equipment inside and out, the new prime movers were not familiar to them, and the Deuce's men did not want to go into combat without knowing the M-5 as well as the old Diamond-T's.

The new sense of urgency was necessary…by the end of the month the 202nd Field Artillery Battalion would be leaving for Normandy, and war.

☆   ☆   ☆

On Friday June 30, 1944, at 0400 hours word came down from Corps Headquarters (Corps HQ) and the alert orders were issued. The men were roused from sleep, tents taken down, loose equipment packed away.

By 0900 the march order was given, and the men of the 202nd Field Artillery Battalion formed-up to leave the alfalfa field that had been their home for seven weeks.

The 961st Field Artillery Battalion, which was also bivouacked in the same field, decided to give the men of the 202nd FA Bn a formal send-off.

"Their commanding officer was Colonel Kaylor," Harold recalls fondly. "He was Regular Army, a graduate of West Point. He got his whole battalion out there and lined them up along the exit road leading from the alfalfa field. They gave us a real nice send-off." (As events would play out, the 961st FA Bn would end up being deployed close to the 202nd FA Bn in Europe, so close, in fact, that Harold remembers his battalion calling in the howitzers of the 961st FA Bn in support of the Deuce's guns).

With their long-awaited call-to-action imminent, the 500 men of the 202nd Field Artillery Battalion bid farewell to their comrades of the 961st FA Bn. Harold and the men loaded into the Deuce's 100-plus vehicles, and with the twelve 155mm howitzers in tow, they headed for their port of embarkation at the docks in Southampton.

While en route to the port Harold observed the vast quantities of men, equipment and supplies that clogged all of the roads leading to the coast, men and material that were also destined for the beaches of Normandy.

For many months prior to June 1944, shipload after shipload of military cargo slated for the invasion had been delivered to ports throughout the United Kingdom. So numerous were the vehicles and mountains of supplies that there simply wasn't enough room to store everything on military bases. Therefore, fields, pastures and meadows across the British Isles were turned into ad hoc supply dumps and motor pools.

As the hour of the invasion neared, many fields began to empty of their vast holdings as the vehicles and shipping crates began making their way to the ports of embarkation. As a result of all of this movement, the narrow British country roads and lanes became a scene of heavy congestion with massed groupings of men, trucks, jeeps and tanks lined up along the roadsides for miles and miles.

"We had a hard time getting to where we needed to be," Harold recalls.

Under a steady rain, the Deuce slowly made its way south, and by evening the battalion eventually arrived in Southhampton.

That night the weather worsened, and as a hard rain fell, the 202nd Field Artillery Battalion drove slowly onto the docks and approached the three LSTs (Landing Ship, Tank) that would carry them across the English Channel.

As the Deuce's vehicles queued-up to commence loading, the LSTs huge bow doors opened, and from each ship a ramp was lowered onto the dock so the vehicles could be driven into the hold of the ship. At this point the soldiers acquiesced to the cargo experts of the U.S. Navy, and the loading process itself was carried out by the sailors on the LSTs.

"Of course we had never seen one of those things up close before," Harold states. "So we let the Navy decide how we would put everything aboard. They were pretty efficient. Those LSTs held a lot of equipment."

Before dawn the following day, the men and equipment of the Deuce were onboard the three ships, all except one howitzer and prime mover, and the gun's crew.

HOWITZERS, GRASSHOPPERS, AND THE HOLY RIGHT HAND

U.S. Army Signal Corps

Men and vehicles load into LSTs at a port in southern England, prior to the voyage across the English Channel to the Normandy beaches. These versatile assault ships carried just about everything, including aircraft (a portion of a wing with the National Insignia is visible behind the truck at the lower left of the photograph).

U.S. Army Signal Corps

When loaded, the Deuce's LSTs appeared similar to this one, with both the lower hold and the upper deck packed with trucks, jeeps, prime movers, howitzers, supplies and men.

"We left them strict orders to join us as soon as they could, to take the next boat over," Harold says. "Somehow they found a spot on a ship and got to Normandy the day after we did," he recalls with a smile.

After rising at 0400 to get the Battalion packed-up, driving all day on congested, wet roads to the coast, and then finally supervising the all-night loading of equipment onto his assigned LST, Harold was understandably exhausted once the loading was completed.

"We were all completely soaked from the rain," he remembers. "The men had to find a place to hunker down with their equipment, and of course I was glad when we got the ship buttoned up so we could go."

"I was walking back and forth on the deck when the captain of the LST told me I'd better get up on his bunk and take a nap because I was useless just walking around...he said I would have plenty to do once we hit the other shore!"

"I was tired, so I did as he recommended and climbed up there on the bunk and slept for several hours. To this day I sure think it was nice of him to give me his bunk so I could get some rest."

★ ★ ★

By dawn on July 1, 1944, the three LSTs carrying the 202nd Field Artillery Battalion had joined their assigned convoy of ships destined for the French coast.

BOGS, RAIN, AND ECHOES OF THE BLITZ

Under dark clouds and a steady rain, the ships swung their bows toward Normandy, increased their speed, and headed out into the choppy, grey waters of the English Channel.

HOWITZERS, GRASSHOPPERS, AND THE HOLY RIGHT HAND

U.S. Army Signal Corps

American GI's on a cart path between two of the ancient Norman hedgerows that were so prevalent inland of the invasion beaches. Judging by the tire tracks in the mud, the path must have been wide enough to allow a jeep to pass through.

Chapter 5

Utah Beach

☆ ☆ ☆ ☆ ☆ ☆ ☆ ☆

Nearly four weeks had passed since June 6, 1944, when the Allies had breached Hitler's Atlantic Wall in Normandy. Allied planners had expected their ground forces to have advanced well into the French interior by this point, but the stiff resistance that was encountered during the initial weeks of fighting forced the planners to consider the possibility that a quick, mobile sweep through France may not happen anytime soon.

In what has been called one of the greatest failures of Allied intelligence during the operational planning for D-Day, the American, British, Canadian and other Allied troops were ill-prepared for maneuvering in the landscape they now found themselves in.

The Normandy countryside just inland from the coast

is composed of basically two types of terrain: marshland and fields. The marshland was impassable, for though men might wade through it, vehicles certainly could not traverse the flooded, soggy ground. The Allied planners knew this, and constructed the overall invasion strategy with the hazards of the marshes in mind: the wet lowlands were to be avoided, with priority given to securing the raised causeways that offered dry passage not only through the marshes, but also over the many streams and irrigation ditches that crossed the area.

The Norman fields, by comparison, were a great surprise to everyone. For hundreds of years, local farmers had partitioned their fields by using hedgerows, very dense plantings which were comprised of massive walls of earth and stone four or five feet tall, and planted with a near-impenetrable growth of bushes and trees that rose up another 15 to 20 feet. As the vegetation had been growing for centuries, their root systems intertwined throughout the earthen mounds, making the hedgerows nearly impossible to breach.

Instead of racing across the French countryside as the invasion planners had envisioned, the Allied soldiers in Normandy found themselves mired in a slow, bloody, agonizing fight in the hedgerows. Safe movement in this hazardous environment required that the men crouch and crawl, always keeping low, for they never knew who or what might be on the other side of the dirt and trees they were huddled up against.

U.S. Army Signal Corps

A team of U.S. Army medics pass a wounded GI over a hedgerow in Normandy.

HOWITZERS, GRASSHOPPERS, AND THE HOLY RIGHT HAND

U.S. Army Signal Corps

The tangled nature of the Norman hedgerows is evident in this photograph, which was taken during the initial weeks of combat in France. The dense plantings are also visible across the field, beyond the two GI's.

Moreover, once they succeeded in taking one field, yet another imposing hedgerow awaited them across the way.

The ancient Norman hedgerows made excellent defensive positions, a deadly quality the Germans clearly realized as they utilized the natural barriers to their benefit time and time again. Defending each mound from well dug-in firing positions, the German troops took a heavy toll on the attacking Allied infantrymen, hammering at them with concentrated rifle, machine gun and mortar fire.

Daily gains for the American GI's and British Tommies were minimal, and many in the Allied camp feared a repeat of the constant bloodletting that was experienced in the stagnant trench warfare of World War I. As in that conflict, any forward momentum had stalled.

The Allied advance in Normandy had bogged down.

★ ★ ★

Utah Beach was the western-most of the five Allied invasion beaches in Normandy. As Harold Brown and the men of the Deuce approached the landing area, they were unaware of the stagnant tactical situation which awaited them in the countryside behind Utah's bluffs.

Unlike "Bloody" Omaha Beach just 15 miles to the east which had been secured by the lives of over a thousand GI's, Utah Beach was, thankfully, the scene of less severe

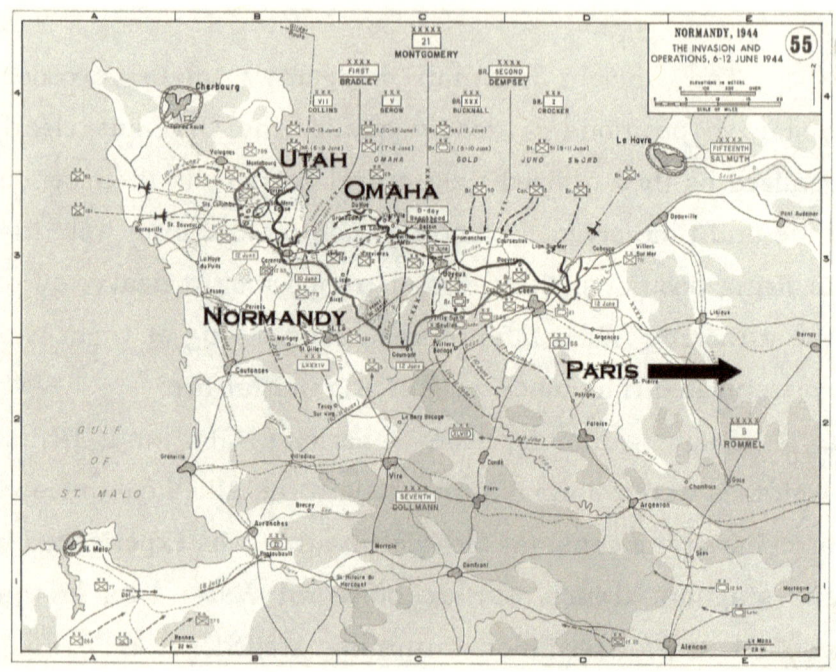

United States Army

Map of the Cotentin Peninsula and the American invasion beaches.

fighting. Still, taking Utah wasn't a cakewalk for the scared, wet and seasick soldiers who made the assault on D-Day, for much American blood was spilled on the sand and rocks there as well; vivid images of which awaited the Deuce.

✯   ✯   ✯

From their station just beyond the coastline of France, the three LSTs carrying the 202nd Field Artillery Battalion waited for the signal to head in to the beachhead. With the massive amounts of men and material pouring over the Channel in a never-ending stream, ship traffic was congested all along the Normandy coast.

Nature, too, had a part to play: there were the tides to consider. At high tide, the LSTs would ground far out from the beach, with hundreds of feet of water between their cargo and the dry sand. If, at that point, the ramps were lowered and the men and vehicles offloaded into the water, they would be required to make a long and dangerous trek to the shore. There were still numerous obstacles and craters, results of the D-Day bombardment and fighting, that were hidden under water at high tide.

Therefore, in order to avoid such hazards, it was decided that it would be better to wait for low tide, so the LSTs would run aground much nearer to the water's edge, with the jeep-swallowing craters and other potential obstacles clearly exposed, and thereby minimizing the dangers they posed to man and machine alike.

HOWITZERS, GRASSHOPPERS, AND THE HOLY RIGHT HAND

As a result of this decision, the Deuce sat off-shore for another 12 hours, waiting for the tide to run out. The men bided their time a little bit longer, more than ready to disembark from the ships and get moving inland.

Finally, on the afternoon of July 2, 1944, the Deuce's LSTs were cleared for the beach. After wallowing offshore for most of the day, the ships screws slowly started to churn, and the big craft moved in towards the French shore.

Though the June 6 battle for the beachhead was long over, evidence of the fighting was still very apparent. Harold describes what he observed from the deck of the LST.

"As we approached the beach we saw many stranded landing craft that had been destroyed on D-Day," he recalls, "and crippled trucks on the beach. I guess there hadn't been time to clear out the damaged equipment, for there was activity everywhere, what with all of the unloading of men and supplies."

What he saw next, though, as his ship ground onto the sand, was a sight he did not expect.

"There were bodies floating in the water...bodies floating," he says quietly. "There were guys out there in motor boats and rowboats, and they were paddling around those floating bodies. The guys had boathooks, and they would reach out and grab the corpses, then pull them into the boats. When they had collected enough to fill the boat, they took the remains to shore where the Graves Registration process was started."

Even though three weeks had passed since D-Day, the waters off of the Normandy coast were still surrendering the bodies of the soldiers and sailors who had been killed there.

Heading to a war zone, Harold and the men of the Deuce knew that in the days ahead they would be seeing bodies of the fallen. But to see them in the waters off of the beach, especially after so much time had passed since the invasion, was very unexpected, and it had a sobering effect on everyone.

"The bodies affected me more than anything," Harold states. "I expected the equipment to be damaged, but I..." He pauses. "I can still remember that as plain as day."

U.S. Army Signal Corps

The soldier nearest the camera looks upon the body of a fallen GI, while the rest of his unit hustles down the road, hugging the edge of the hedgerow.

Chapter 6

Danger in the Hedgerows
Grasshoppers in the Sky

★ ★ ★ ★ ★ ★ ★ ★

By the time the 202nd Field Artillery Battalion hit the shore of Normandy, the front line had advanced fifteen miles inland, nearly half-way across the neck of the Cotentin Peninsula. Yet the front was still close enough for the men to hear the sounds of artillery fire, an ominous portent of the days to come.

With the distant booming in their ears, Harold and his fellow artillerymen left their vantage points along the ship's railings, and proceeded to their vehicles to prepare for disembarking.

Ready to unload their human and mechanical cargo, the LSTs opened their huge bow doors, lowered ramps, and

National Archives

Two LSTs on the beach in Normandy. The Deuce would cross the English Channel in three of these craft.

the GI's of the Deuce drove through the lapping waves of low tide and onto the firm sand of the beach.

After 1,148 days of field maneuvers, extensive training and schooling, Captain Harold E. Brown, United States Army, was going into combat.

☆ ☆ ☆

In order to quickly clear the beach for the next wave of unloading, the 202nd FA Bn efficiently marshaled their many vehicles, and were immediately directed to the nearest exit that led through the bluffs overlooking Utah Beach. Joining the long, congested procession of soldiers and vehicles leaving the landing zone, the artillerymen drove up the sandy road through the bluff, and headed slowly across the causeway that led inland.

In single file on the narrow French roads, the Deuce drove as quickly as possible through the towns of Ravenoville and Ste-Mère-Eglise, coming to a halt a few miles from the latter at a site designated for de-waterproofing the equipment.

"Back in Wheatley we had put this putty-like stuff over the spark plugs and other components to waterproof the vehicles," Harold says. "In fact I could drive my jeep completely submerged because it had a tailpipe that came out the back and went up a few feet. As long as it had that tailpipe open, and everything else was sealed, if the water got deeper than the jeep we could just go right on through."

U.S. Army Signal Corps

A view from one of the exits off of Utah Beach. Numerous Allied landing craft and ships are visible off-shore in the waters of the English Channel.

U.S. Army Signal Corps

Atop the bluffs behind Utah Beach, masses of men and equipment make their way inland after the D-Day invasion. Harold Brown and the Deuce traveled this route on July 2, 1944.

U.S. Army Signal Corps

As Harold Brown observed, destroyed vehicles, ranging from German halftracks to American Sherman tanks, line the side of a road in Normandy.

U.S. Army Signal Corps

A destroyed German Panther tank along the side of a road in Normandy, being examined by what appear to be Army Air Force personnel. The extreme height of the hedgerows is apparent in this photograph, as even the individual sitting on the turret would not be able to see over the wall of earth and plantings.

"But we never got quite that deep. When we drove off of the LST ramp I got my feet wet...my driver stood on his seat and drove from up there. It wasn't too bad, though. We just moved right along."

And they kept moving right along, even before the current task was complete. The order came down to move out immediately, so the artillerymen halted the de-waterproofing process, and headed northwest without delay.

★ ★ ★

While en route to the assigned area, the Deuce's convoy passed countless reminders of the initial battles for Normandy.

"Shell holes were everywhere," Harold states, "and we passed many shot up trucks. It was a real wreck along the roads."

Parachutes still hung from trees, and wrecked gliders were everywhere, remnants of the airborne assault phase of operation OVERLORD.

Harold continues, "The fields where the gliders landed were a mess. The Germans had planted poles in the ground that would rip off the wings as the gliders landed, and the pilots couldn't avoid them. Many of the gliders were just destroyed."

The Battalion moved past many scenes similar to these, the men slowly taking it all in, eventually arriving at their destination, about a mile from the front line.

U.S. Army Signal Corps

An Allied Horsa glider that came to rest on a low hedgerow in Normandy. After the nighttime jump by Allied paratroopers in the predawn hours of D-Day, gliders were utilized to deliver reinforcements, jeeps and light artillery during the daylight hours of June 6, 1944. Harold Brown has vivid recollections of the remnants of the airborne phase of Operation OVERLORD that he viewed in Normandy.

Photograph by Third Signal Company.   Courtesy of dogfacesoldiers.org

WACO *gliders were scattered profusely throughout the fields and meadows of Normandy during the invasion. Landing in one of these wood and canvas craft was hazardous enough when conditions were perfect, let alone in a combat zone that was populated by numerous anti-glider obstacles. Many of the* WACO *and* Horsa *gliders were destroyed upon landing, killing and injuring many of the glider troops they were carrying.*

DANGER IN THE HEDGEROWS, GRASSHOPPERS IN THE SKY

No longer distant rumblings, the sounds of battle were all too clear now.

★   ★   ★

Within nine hours of coming ashore, the howitzers of the 202nd Field Artillery Battalion were set up in a field just north of the little town of Vindefontaine, firing a few rounds into enemy territory to register the guns.

"Our shells had a range of about nine miles, but we didn't often fire that far because the howitzer would really boom with all of that powder in there. It was harder on the weapon," Harold explains.

The firing process for the 155mm howitzers was a bit more involved than for artillery that used shells with their own attached metal powder casing.

"The loader would bring a shell over, just the explosive shell, and it was rammed into the breach," Harold continues. "Next the powder charge was put in. It came in increments, in cloth bags, charge one through seven or eight. So if you needed charge five, you removed the increments that were extra. We just loaded enough powder to reach the target."

"We would dig a large pit for the extra charge bags, pile them up in the hole, and eventually burn them," he says. Not, however, until it was safe to do so.

The Germans had observation posts and snipers all over the Norman countryside. If they weren't careful, the

GI's would soon be on the receiving end of sniper fire or incoming artillery rounds, a lesson that many times was learned the hard way. It didn't take long for Harold to see an example of this.

"On one of my first few days in Normandy, I went through a hedgerow," he recalls, "and I saw a lieutenant laying there…flat on his back with his arms out…and of course he was dead, a victim of a sniper."

Scenes such as this were observed many times, and as a result, American soldiers learned to take proactive measures in order to prevent a dangerous or deadly incident from occurring in the first place.

"Sometimes we would meet up with some paratroopers," Harold continues, "and if they saw a tree that was thick with foliage, they would take their machine guns and sweep the tree with fire in case any snipers were hidden up there. Those guys didn't take any chances."

"It was also known that the snipers would single out officers, ignoring the enlisted men. I was aware of this as I had my captain's bars on the front of my helmet."

"So I took some of our waterproofing putty and put it over the bars so they wouldn't show. Now Patton, being a real stickler for regulations, wouldn't have liked this, but I thought it was a good idea!"

★ ★ ★

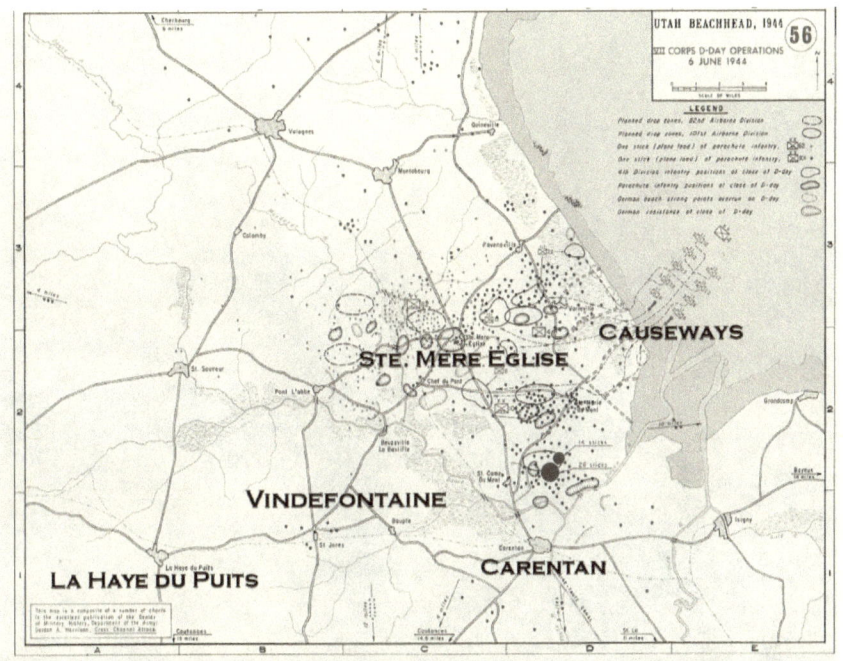

United States Army

Map of Normandy, France. Utah Beach Sector.

The 202nd Field Artillery Battalion exited the beachhead via one of the causeways, then passed through Ste-Mère-Eglise on their way to Vindefontaine.

Harold Brown's initial Grasshopper flights were in the vicinity of the towns of La Haye-du-Puits and Carentan.

U.S. Army Signal Corps

A 155mm howitzer engaged in a fire mission in Normandy. Harold Brown relates that the tarps and camouflage nets pictured above were employed more frequently during the early stages of the European campaign. Many times the Deuce didn't stay in one location long enough to make setting-up the coverings worthwhile.

Hiding your insignia may have worked for snipers, but it didn't help at all when it came to land mines and enemy artillery, both of which were plentiful among the hedgerows. During his first two weeks in France, Harold had close calls with both.

"One day we were going one way on a road, and another outfit had sent a jeep coming back the other way," he relates. "Well, when he got right beside us, he hit a mine."

"The explosion was deafening, and everything turned black...totally black. You couldn't even see the dashboard on our jeep."

"All of that stuff that had been blown upwards started coming down on us. Of course my driver had to stop because he couldn't see where he was going."

"When the smoke and debris cleared, we had large chunks of asphalt sitting on the hood of our jeep, and the jeep that hit the mine was on the other side of the road. I looked over by it and saw a soldier coming up out of the ditch beside the road, and I asked him if he was alone or if he had people with him. He was pretty shook up, but he said he was by himself."

"Then I looked out in the field beyond him and his jeep, and there was one of those quarter-ton trailers, lying upside down, with its wheels still turning around and around."

HOWITZERS, GRASSHOPPERS, AND THE HOLY RIGHT HAND

U.S. Army Signal Corps

A U.S. Army jeep maneuvers in the muck between hedgerows in Normandy.

Photograph courtesy of Rich Heller   warfoto.com

Pictured are jeeps and ¼ ton trailers similar to the one that hit a mine beside Harold Brown's jeep.

HOWITZERS, GRASSHOPPERS, AND THE HOLY RIGHT HAND

A close call for sure, and Harold recalls another encounter he experienced shortly after arriving in Normandy.

"On just our second or third day ashore," he begins, "I was out scouting with my assistant, First Sergeant Merle Jones. It was my responsibility for finding routes for the battalion to go from one place to another, so Sgt. Jones and I were out front, doing just that."

"We had parked our jeep behind a hedgerow, along with the ¾ ton truck that held all of the equipment for our survey section, items like our transit, aiming circle and whatnot."

"Jones and I were on foot and had crossed to the far side of the hedgerow when all of a sudden the Germans started shelling us...with 88's," (the German's high-velocity 88mm gun was the most-feared artillery piece in the Nazi's arsenal).

"Of course with metal shrapnel whizzing by, you look for the lowest place you can find," Harold explains. "You try to expose as little of your body as possible, so I flopped down in a little depression."

"Well, one of those shells came in and hit about 15 or 20 yards from me, and it just turned me *completely* over...shook me from lying on my stomach to lying on my back."

"The shelling continued on for about...well...it seemed like a lifetime...but it was actually just four or five minutes during which they shot in 15 or 20 shells over that area. We could hear them coming each time as the 88's had a peculiar whistle."

"Finally, though, the Germans shifted fire to another target, and things quieted down."

Hopeful that the shelling had ended, Harold decided to raise his head up out of the depression to see what happened to Merle Jones.

"Sgt. Jones was lying over there face down," Harold relates, "and he had his helmet on with his arms lying in front of his face, protecting himself."

"He lifts his head and says, 'Captain, how many places would you rather be than right here?'"

Here the story pauses, and Harold gets a big smile on his face.

"I thought to myself, 'There are a *lot* of places I'd rather be than here!'"

"That was probably the closest I ever came to getting it with an artillery shell," Harold says. "During my time in Europe we had an awful lot of enemy shells fall on our area, but never *that* close. That was near enough that if I had been standing up, I never would have made it because the shrapnel was flying all over."

The hedgerows, though a bane to the Allies for mobility reasons, did have a benefit in that they offered good protection while under artillery fire.

"If I was in a hedgerow," Harold states, "the only way they could get me is a direct hit. That would have finished

Harold Brown Collection

First Sergeant Merle Jones, who along with Harold Brown ducked German 88's that were targeting the two of them in the Norman hedgerow in July 1944.

me off. You would just try to get on either side of a hedgerow when the shells started falling."

This is also when Harold shares his thoughts on how he managed to survive the war without serious injury.

"It was just luck," he says. "I've been asked that many, many times, how I escaped the war without getting seriously hit. And I always say it was just luck."

"I never knew which side of the hedgerow to get behind; I just got to what ever cover I could find."

The shelling that day wasn't entirely without results, however. Beyond the hedgerow where Harold and Merle Jones had taken cover, one of the German shells scored a direct hit on the ¾ ton truck that belonged to the battalion survey section, wrecking it and everything it was hauling.

As if losing all of the survey equipment wasn't bad enough, Harold and Merle had to hit the dirt again because members of the survey crew had decided to collect abandoned German machine gun ammunition belts, which they chose to display by draping the belts all over the sides of the truck. Therefore, it wasn't long until the rounds started to cook-off in the fire of the burning truck.

"I certainly didn't want to get hit by any of those!" Harold says.

Once it was safe to get up, Harold and Merle went to check out the shell holes the 88's had left.

Photograph by Third Signal Company.   Courtesy of dogfacesoldiers.org

When a German 88mm shell meets a jeep.

DANGER IN THE HEDGEROWS, GRASSHOPPERS IN THE SKY

"When a shell hits, it leaves a furrow, a shiny trail of earth on the back of the hole as it enters the ground, similar to what a spade makes when you dig," Harold explains. "From the furrow we could tell what direction the shell came from."

"We had a shell report that we sent in to Corps headquarters. Anybody who got shelled was required to send in a shelling report."

"As Corps gets all of these shell reports, they draw lines on a map for each one. The plotters could then trace back on that azimuth, and, by using triangulation, they could determine where there might be a battery. Then they can call in artillery or the Air Corps so they can smash it."

Of course what worked for the Americans also worked for the Germans; the Deuce's fire could give away their own position. Consequently, sometimes after completing a fire mission, the Deuce would shift to either side of its position, hopefully in enough time to avoid any retaliatory fire from German artillery. Such moves were added work for the gun crews, but the benefits far outweighed the hassles, so nobody complained.

★   ★   ★

German artillery fire, especially from the 88mm FlaK guns, was naturally a source of great concern to the men of the Deuce.

The Luftwaffe by comparison was not a source of great worry among Harold and his fellow GI's. The once-feared German air force, nearly swept from the skies of France by this stage of the war, usually made its appearance only at night.

"Washing Machine Charlie we called him," Harold says, "due to all of the racket he made. He'd fly over us every night and randomly drop a few bombs to harass us. He'd wake us up, but it was no big deal."

It was also during these early days in combat that Harold returned the favor of harassing the enemy by flying low over German lines himself. He, however, directed fire on the Wehrmacht that was much more devastating than the few random bombs dropped by Washing Machine Charlie.

"When you're a forward observer," Harold explains, "you can direct fire much more quickly and accurately from the air as opposed to when you are on the ground where you have to push your way through brush and maneuver over visual obstacles like hills. Air spotters are a lot more effective."

His first few missions involved flights over enemy positions south of the towns of Carentan and La Haye-du-Puits, the latter of which was 16 miles west of Carentan along the D903 highway; the Americans were still hemmed-in at Normandy, and Harold did not have far to fly to see the German positions.

DANGER IN THE HEDGEROWS, GRASSHOPPERS IN THE SKY

U.S. Army Signal Corps

An aerial view of the Norman countryside. The extent of the hedgerows is readily apparent in this view, as is the value of observation from the air. Harold Brown experienced similar views many times on his observing/spotting missions in Normandy.

HOWITZERS, GRASSHOPPERS, AND THE HOLY RIGHT HAND

Unlike the much larger and heavier fighter-type aircraft that were also employed for reconnaissance, the little Piper Cub L-4 "Grasshoppers" were able to take off and land from small fields. They did not require landing strips or vast quantities of support equipment.

Nor, however, did they offer much in the way of protection from enemy fire.

Flying from just a few hundred to a couple of thousand feet off of the ground, the slow-moving, fabric-covered airplanes were enticing targets for the German anti-aircraft gunners and riflemen down below, as well as for the occasional German fighter that managed to avoid the swarms of Allied aircraft patrolling above the French countryside.

Harold would rotate through the spotting missions along with the five or six other forward observers in the battalion.

"We had two spotter aircraft assigned to our battalion along with two pilots," Harold says. "In addition to myself there were two regular forward observers and three lieutenants who were forward observers for each of the three batteries. All of us would take turns flying the missions."

"Now, the pilots were also trained as spotters, but if they concentrated on directing fire there would be no one to watch out for enemy planes. So we would do the spotting while the pilot flew the pattern and kept his eyes open for German aircraft."

Photograph by Third Signal Company.   Courtesy of dogfacesoldiers.org

The light construction of the Grasshopper observation airplane is evidenced in this photograph. Harold Brown completed over 50 missions in these dependable, but slow, canvas-covered airplanes.

HOWITZERS, GRASSHOPPERS, AND THE HOLY RIGHT HAND

"Once over enemy territory, I would fold down the side window, brace my arms on the side of the door, and scan the ground with my field glasses looking for targets."

Harold describes this in a matter-of-fact-way, but flying the missions was actually very dangerous business. Flying low and slow, his plane was frequently a target for the German troops on the ground below.

"My first time up in Normandy, the Germans were shooting at us with pistols and rifles because we were so close to the ground," he relates.

"They shot holes in our wings. You could hear the bullets going through the fabric, like when you go target shooting and you hear the bullet "snap" through the target."

When asked how this made him feel, to have someone shooting directly at him, Harold simply says, "I just wanted to get on with the mission and get it over with."

Being in an unarmed aircraft, though, wasn't it at least a little exasperating not being able to hit back?

"Oh, I could get back at them," he answers wryly.

After all, those 155mm howitzers had a long reach!

★   ★   ★

For the Allied soldiers, combat in the hedgerows progressed at a snail's pace throughout July 1944. It was hazardous, costly fighting, with hidden dangers as well.

DANGER IN THE HEDGEROWS, GRASSHOPPERS IN THE SKY

"One of my jobs was to warn the troops of the booby traps," Harold explains. "The Germans would set a *lot* of booby traps."

"You'd see a pistol lying on the ground, and the natural thing to do is to step over and pick it up. Well, it could be booby trapped."

"One day we were between two hedgerows, going up and down the ditch between them, and here's this gun barrel sticking out of the bank of the ditch. It looked enticing for somebody who was curious. So I told the troops, 'Avoid that thing,' and they all stepped around it."

"After we were all clear of it, we tied a long rope on it and pulled, and sure enough it was booby trapped. It exploded and probably would have killed three or four people."

"You had to be really careful. They had various things like cameras, lying around so they could be seen. You'd stop to pick one up, and 'BOOM!'"

"So we tried to teach these guys to keep their hands off of stuff like that."

Advance was cautious and slow as a result of the various dangers present in Normandy. Like all soldiers who desired to make it through to the next day, Harold paid close attention to his surroundings, taking care not to repeat mistakes that others had made at the cost of life or limb.

HOWITZERS, GRASSHOPPERS, AND THE HOLY RIGHT HAND

During the initial few weeks in action, he and his fellow artillerymen became further accustomed each day to the sights and sounds of combat. To improve their chances of survival, they quickly learned how to behave and react effectively in hazardous situations.

With their eyes open for snipers, booby traps and land mines, their movement organized to avoid enemy artillery, and their sleep disrupted by a lone German airplane, the men of the Deuce made it through their first month in combat.

During that time their twelve howitzers fired 7,588 rounds at the enemy.

Before leaving Europe, they would fire over 54,000 more.

U.S. Army Signal Corps

Combat in the hedgerows of Normandy. The GI in the center of the photograph appears to be firing a rifle grenade over the dense foliage. Fighting was difficult and confused in such surroundings, where vision was limited and movement impaired.

HOWITZERS, GRASSHOPPERS, AND THE HOLY RIGHT HAND

U.S. Army Signal Corps

A U.S. Army 155mm howitzer heading down a Norman road, towed behind an M-5 prime mover.

U.S. Army Signal Corps

A close-up of the photograph on the preceding page. This is the "comfortable" transportation, whether in sun, rain or snow, afforded to the GI's in the Army Artillery. They would tell you that it sure beats walking, though! Might these artillerymen belong to the Deuce?

U.S. Army Signal Corps

Lieutenant General Omar N. Bradley, Commander of the U.S. First Army. Bradley's Operation COBRA effected the Allied breakout from Normandy.

Chapter 7

COBRA and Tigers

☆ ☆ ☆ ☆ ☆ ☆ ☆ ☆

In late July 1944, with hopes of breaking through the German lines and ending the stalemate in Normandy, the Allies launched a new offensive: Operation COBRA.

The man tasked with COBRA's execution was Lieutenant General Omar N. Bradley, commander of the U.S. First Army.

Known as "The Soldier's General" due to the high regard and compassion that he held for the GI's under his command, Bradley hoped to move the American ground forces out of the killing zones of the hedgerows and into the open countryside where the highly-mechanized Allies could then maneuver more freely against the Germans.

Rather than a broad push against the entire main line of resistance, COBRA would hit the Germans along a

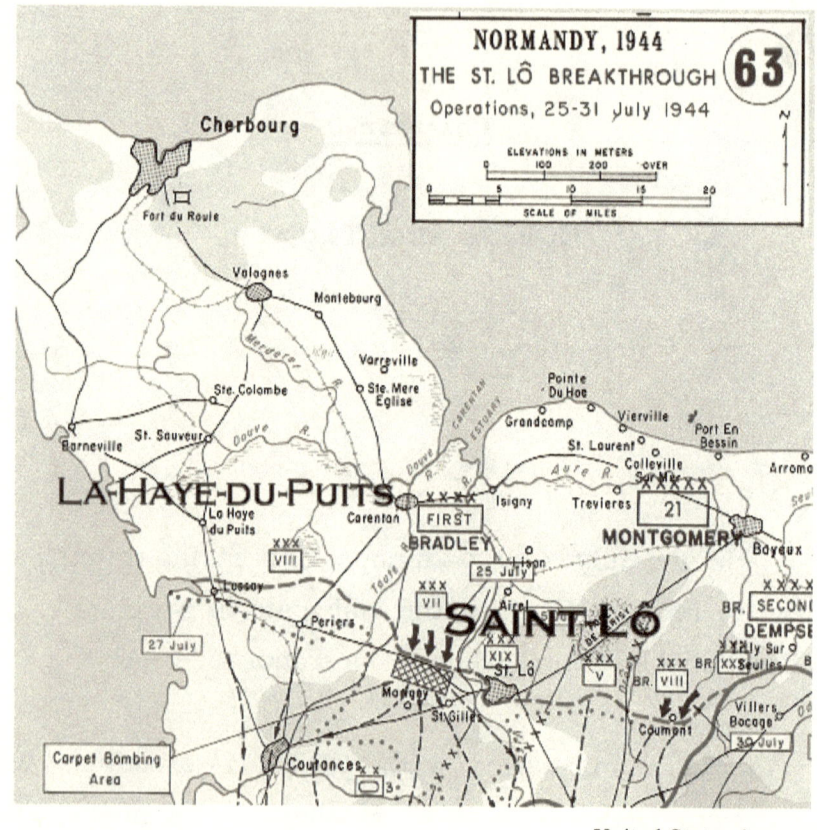

United States Army

Operation COBRA, the Allied Breakout from Normandy

The dashed line running east-west through Saint-Lô depicts the stagnant front line that penned-in the Allied forces for many weeks after D-Day. COBRA's aim was to breach the German line at two focused points, notated by the small black arrows to the east and west of Saint-Lô.

narrow front, with a massive, focused push to break-open the enemy defenses.

The jump-off point was from a line running roughly east and west of the strategic crossroads city of Saint-Lô, located 18 miles southeast of Carentan. Using the road network emanating from rubble-strewn Saint-Lô, Bradley hoped American armor would quickly advance through the German line and head southeast into the heart of France.

★   ★   ★

COBRA's assault on the enemy line of defense began with a massive aerial bombardment by U.S. Army Air Force heavy bombers, followed by an intense artillery barrage that pummeled the German soldiers huddling in their shelters and foxholes. Under this terrific pounding the enemy line lost its cohesiveness, and American and British troops surged through weakened sections of the German defenses.

By the end of July, COBRA's initial goal of ending the stalemate in Normandy was realized as Bradley's attack rapidly progressed. The Allies were finally on the move.

On Aug. 1, 1944, sensing that the time was right, Supreme Allied Commander General Dwight D. Eisenhower put into action the man who would push and harass the Germans incessantly until the end of hostilities: Lieutenant General George S. Patton.

U.S. Army Signal Corps

U.S. Army vehicles roll through devastated Saint-Lô, France. The Allies repeatedly targeted the strategic crossroads town in an effort to dislodge the German defenders. As a result of the pounding, nearly every building in the city was destroyed or damaged.

National Archives

Ike and his generals.
General Dwight D. Eisenhower (seated, 4th from left).
General George S. Patton (seated, 2nd from left).
General Omar N. Bradley (seated, 5th from left).

HOWITZERS, GRASSHOPPERS, AND THE HOLY RIGHT HAND

Like Bradley, Patton was, with some exceptions, respected by the men who served under his command. Unlike Bradley, Patton wasn't known for his compassion.

In the eyes of many of the GI's, however, he made up for this shortcoming by his single-minded focus on the battle, to keep hitting, keep pushing, to show no mercy to the enemy. Keep them off-balance and on the run, and you will minimize casualties. Give the enemy time to regroup and entrench, and casualties will increase.

Patton also greatly endeared himself to his men by being out in the field with them, showing himself in places where many Allied commanders would never allow themselves to be found. Not content with remaining in a "safe" HQ miles behind the action, Patton much preferred to be close to the battle.

This was the case in early August 1944, as Patton and his U.S. Third Army hit the ground running with a vengeance.

★   ★   ★

As for Harold Brown and the 202nd Field Artillery Battalion, when operation COBRA commenced they found themselves 27 miles northwest of Carentan, in the town of Bricquebec.

Temporarily removed from the front line, the Deuce was finally able to attend to the de-waterproofing of their equipment, four weeks after coming ashore. The battalion had been in action continually since arriving in France, and a brief lull allowed the men to complete this task.

The break in action was indeed short-lived however, for on August 2, 1944, the Deuce was assigned to Patton and his U.S. Third Army. Orders came through attaching the 202nd FA Bn to an armored column headed by the 5th Armored Division. The breakout from Normandy was underway.

Instead of daily progress along the combat front being measured in yards as was often the case in Normandy, the Allies would now be moving the front line forward many miles each day, sometimes tens of miles.

As part of this offensive, the Deuce was no exception. They would travel over 540 miles by the end of the month, but not before taking part in the destruction of German Army Group B in the Falaise Pocket.

★   ★   ★

Howitzers in tow, the 202nd Field Artillery Battalion joined-up with the tanks and mechanized infantry of the 5th Armored Division. Under Patton's direction, the men headed south, first paralleling the western coast of the Cotentin Peninsula, then swinging to the southeast toward the city of Le Mans.

All through this advance, the Americans were greeted as victors by jubilant French men and women as town after

HOWITZERS, GRASSHOPPERS, AND THE HOLY RIGHT HAND

town was liberated from the Nazi oppressors. For the most part the French civilians were ecstatic to see the GI's. Bottles of wine and cognac were plentiful, as were kisses from French girls and women.

Harold, being occupied with the movement of the battalion, didn't get much of a chance to partake in these spoils for the victors. However he does recall the contact that he had with one group of French civilians, the children.

After relieving the GI's of gum and candy, the French children would assist in the gathering of intelligence.

"Unlike many of the adults, the kids could speak English as they studied it in school," Harold explains. "They could translate for us. We'd ask the grownups questions, such as how long ago were the Germans here, and how many, etc. The kids would translate for us, so we ended up getting some useful information that way."

Most of the time, however, the information was too old to be relevant as the Germans were rapidly falling back, reeling from the Allied offensive.

★ ★ ★

The tactical situation on the ground was now very fluid, changing day by day as the Allies pushed further and further into France. During this time the men of the Deuce utilized their months of training, repeatedly deploying the howitzers for fire missions, then quickly packing up and getting back on the road.

"All those cannoneers had a job to do when we stopped," Harold explains. "First the battalion executive officer would give them a line of fire so they could set their sites. Then they'd get a base deflection, which was a line that they would shift fire from, right or left. After that the howitzers were ready to fire on the register point."

"The whole process took only 30 minutes," he continues, "and in fact we could do it quicker than that if we had to. Those howitzers are pretty big weapons, but ten men on the trails (the metal split-arms of the gun carriage that extend to the rear of the howitzer) could swing one around pretty quickly."

Being able to deploy the howitzers so rapidly was valuable in most combat situations, but not when faced with thick-skinned German armor.

"We'd be moving along, scanning the area out in front of us and every so often we'd see tanks," Harold remembers, "sometimes Tiger tanks."

The German Tiger tank was a 60 ton behemoth, over 50,000 pounds heavier than the American main battle tank, the Sherman, and the GI's feared it.

"The tanks would be moving away from us or moving across our front," he recalls. "You'd hope they would fall back, but sometimes they'd stand and shoot at us."

If the batteries were deployed, the Deuce could fire back at the enemy armor. Against smaller and lightly-armored German *Panzers*, the Battalion's guns achieved

HOWITZERS, GRASSHOPPERS, AND THE HOLY RIGHT HAND

U.S. Army Signal Corps

A German Panzerkampfwagen VI Tiger tank.
Heavily armored and equipped with the powerful 88mm gun, this heavy tank was extremely difficult to destroy. American infantrymen, artillerymen and armor crews respected and feared the Tiger. The Tiger pictured above was captured intact.

U.S. Army Signal Corps

The effectiveness of the thick frontal armor on German tanks is apparent in this photograph of a Pzkw Mark V Panther. Six American shells ricocheted off of the sloping armor before the seventh shell penetrated at the seam between the upper and lower hulls.

some success, disabling and destroying a number of enemy tanks.

Tigers were a different story, however; the Deuce's return fire was useless against the huge German tanks.

"Our howitzer shells were not effective against them at all," Harold explains. "They'd just bounce off a Tiger's armor."

The German heavy tank was protected by 4 inches of armor up front; by comparison the U.S. Sherman had but 2 ½ inches protecting it.

"We'd put a call out for our tanks through the phone network," Harold continues, "and some Shermans would show up."

"Usually it took a number of our tanks to defeat one German tank. The German shells would go right through a Sherman, so we'd have to put a few Shermans on a Tiger to chase it off or to hit it from behind and destroy it."

The Tiger, and the equally feared German Panther medium tank, were both armed with high-velocity main guns; the dreaded 88mm in the Tiger, and an equally effective 75mm in the Panther. Either tank could fire armor-piercing rounds that would penetrate a Sherman's armor from a much greater distance than the closer range that was required of the lower-velocity Sherman 75mm gun. Like most GI's, Harold had a healthy respect for the big German armor.

"That would terrorize you more than anything, those Tiger tanks," Harold claims.

Photograph by Third Signal Company. Courtesy of dogfacesoldiers.org

The U.S. Sherman tank.

Although not as well armed or armored as the German Panther and Tiger tanks, the Sherman nonetheless prevailed in the end due to its speed, greater reliability, and, most importantly, sheer numbers manufactured. American factories mass-produced Shermans so successfully, combat losses were easily replaced. Unfortunately, the same could not be said for the trained tank crewmen. U.S. armor crews suffered terrible losses, and many times Shermans were manned in combat by fewer than the five crewmen the tank was designed to hold.

Photograph by Third Signal Company. Courtesy of dogfacesoldiers.org

Far too many Sherman tanks suffered a fate similar to this one.

HOWITZERS, GRASSHOPPERS, AND THE HOLY RIGHT HAND

National Archives

Nearest the camera, from the left: Patton, Bradley and Montgomery. That Bradley is pictured between two of the biggest egos in World War II is most appropriate. There was no love lost between Patton and Montgomery.

Chapter 8

Death in the Gap

★ ★ ★ ★ ★ ★ ★ ★

By the end of the first week of August 1944, there developed on General Bradley's planning maps what appeared to be an opportunity to deal the Germans a crushing blow.

The enemy's line was bulged, anchored on the north just outside of Caen, then running southwest towards the coast.

Approximately 25 miles from the coast the line turned sharply back about 150 degrees, and ran southeast to Le Mans.

This formed a well-defined bulge, with British Field Marshall Bernard L. Montgomery's I Corps on the northern shoulder near Falaise, and Patton's U.S. Third Army at the southern shoulder, pushing north from Le Mans to the city of Argentan.

If the two opposing Allied armies could push towards each other and meet, an entire German Army Group would be trapped in the bulge.

Over the next week, however, the Allies applied pressure all along the German lines, with the effect that the bulge soon shrank in size to that of a smaller enclosed area, a "pocket" that was approximately 15 miles wide and 20 miles deep at the extremes, but with a narrow neck of approximately eight miles width through which the Germans were fleeing to the east.

Due to the terrain of the area, escape routes through the neck were limited, and with over 100,000 Wehrmacht soldiers and thousands of vehicles clogging the roads, Allied aircraft and artillery had many more targets than they could possibly hope to destroy.

The men of the Deuce called this area the Argentan Gap, but the battle became forever known as the Falaise Gap.

And it was a killing ground.

"We set up our batteries on a hill looking down into the Gap," Harold recalls. The 202nd Field Artillery Battalion had moved up to a location near the small town of Nonant-le-Pin, about ten miles east of Argentan and directly below the neck of the Gap.

"I sat there for two days and directed fire at the Germans," he relates. "I was up on a hill watching, and I could see them real well."

"Of course that meant they could see us, too! We had to hide the men and howitzers, keep them out of sight, because the Germans would spot you and send counter fire at you. So we kept our heads down and tried to keep a line of vision into the Gap."

"I had a telephone that was connected to Battalion HQ," Harold continues, "and every time a target would appear we would fire on them. Targets were plentiful as the Germans were disorganized and trying to escape. They were everywhere down there, moving in broad daylight. I think they knew what they were in for."

By this point in the battle, the Deuce had advanced in front of the American armor and the supporting infantry. Consequently, they were exposed at the point of the advance, without a buffer of infantry between their howitzers and the Germans.

The Germans, however, were more intent on escaping than they were on attacking, and the howitzers of the 202nd FA Bn fired day and night for 48 hours.

"I don't know how many we killed, but it was *thousands*," Harold says. "They couldn't get out."

★ ★ ★

HOWITZERS, GRASSHOPPERS, AND THE HOLY RIGHT HAND

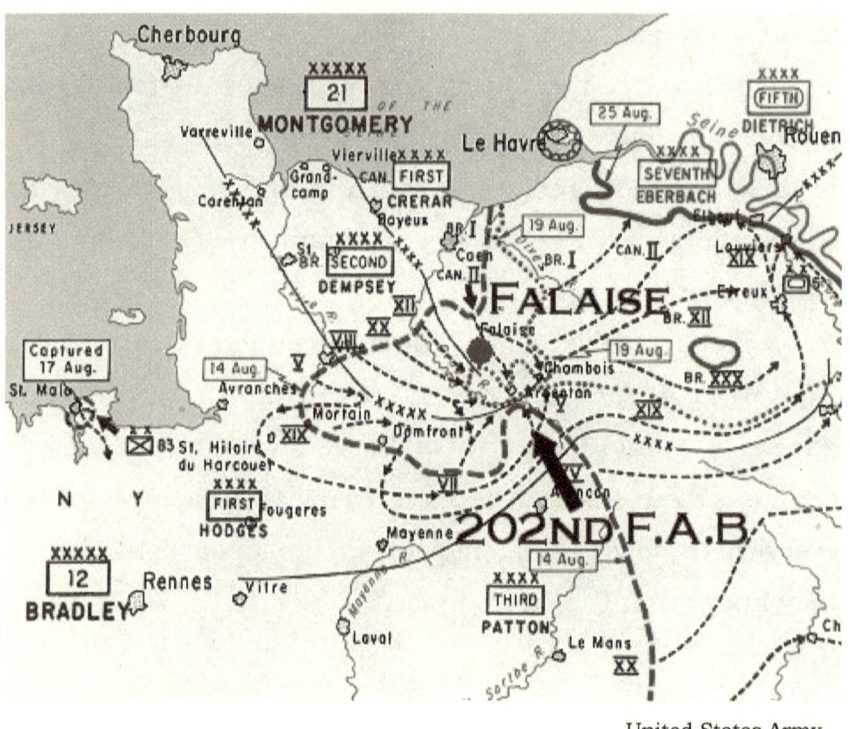

United States Army

The pocket of Germans trapped near Falaise is notated by the thick, dashed line on the map. The "Gap", between the two black arrows, grew increasingly narrow as the British and Canadians pushed south, and as Patton's GI's pushed north. Harold Brown and the Deuce were on a hilltop near the point of the lower arrow, raining shells down on the thousands of Wehrmacht troops in the valley below.

DEATH IN THE GAP

U.S. Army Signal Corps

Death and destruction in the Falaise Gap. With tens of thousands of men and vehicles crowded into such a small area, the Germans suffered horrendous losses at the hands of Allied artillery and airpower.

HOWITZERS, GRASSHOPPERS, AND THE HOLY RIGHT HAND

By August 20-21, 1944, Patton's GI's pushing up from the south met Montgomery's men advancing down from the north, and the Falaise Gap was sealed off. Tens of thousands of Germans had escaped, but tens of thousands more were also killed or captured.

The Gap itself was a macabre landscape of unimaginable death and destruction as the dead lay unburied and the sides of the roads were clogged with destroyed vehicles and equipment.

Harold and the 202nd Field Artillery Battalion passed through the Gap on their way to resuming the dash across France. Harold remembers one scene in particular that has stuck with him.

"My driver and I were passing through the Falaise Gap as part of the American column that was pursuing the retreating Germans," he recalls. "The Germans were horse-drawn; they had hundreds and hundreds of horses to pull their weapons and wagons, and of course a lot of the horses were killed."

"We were going through that mess to get on down towards Paris when we drove around a white horse; he was close enough that I could reach out and touch him as the jeep went by. The rest of the horses were mixed colors, but the white one stood out. He was the only white horse I saw along the road."

60 years later, Harold was watching a video program of the battle that included film footage taken along the very

road he traveled, and sure enough, there was the white horse, in the same position as the one he saw, dead along the side of the road.

"I knew *right* where that was," he says.

HOWITZERS, GRASSHOPPERS, AND THE HOLY RIGHT HAND

National Archives

Lieutenant General George S. Patton.

Yes, he was as tough as he looks.

Chapter 9

Patton Races for Paris

★ ★ ★ ★ ★ ★ ★ ★

With the breakout from Normandy now complete, the men of the Deuce left the Falaise Gap behind and joined in the race across the interior of France.

"We took off from there," Harold relates, "and we were going pretty fast, we really picked up speed."

★ ★ ★

"Patton, of course, had to do his own thing, and he was out ahead of the other divisions on our right and left flanks," Harold explains. "So that put us in a "finger" of territory that didn't have any protection on either side. We were pretty exposed, but we weren't frightened because we had the Germans pretty well disorganized."

HOWITZERS, GRASSHOPPERS, AND THE HOLY RIGHT HAND

Patton was in his element, pushing his troops forward, with the Germans on the run in front of his rapidly pursuing Third Army.

GI's who served under Patton have many stories about him directing traffic along the roads of Europe, waving them on, urging them to keep after the enemy. Such appearances were unusual for a general, but not for Patton. His men loved it, and they really appreciated seeing him out in the field with them.

Harold saw Patton six or seven times during the two months that the 202nd Field Artillery Battalion was under operational command of "Georgie", as his men often referred to him. Harold also vividly remembers Patton directing traffic along the roads in France as the Deuce rolled past.

"He was out there directing traffic, standing there like a goof, waving us on, clapping his hands, wearing his ivory-handled revolvers," recalls Harold, gesticulating in imitation of Patton. "He was out where the action was, so we got to see him quite a few times."

Constantly urged forward, the GI's of the Third Army did as Patton directed, pushing to the east as rapidly as possible. So rapidly in fact, that the lead units advanced into areas beyond the maps they were issued. Such was the case with Harold and the Deuce.

"I was up in the spotter plane in late-August, and we had run off of the maps they had issued to us," he states.

Photograph by Third Signal Company.   Courtesy of dogfacesoldiers.org

The retreating Germans destroyed most bridges in front of the advancing Americans. Further progress was delayed until the U.S. Army Engineers could erect a temporary span, such as this Bailey Bridge over a French river.

"Somehow I got hold of a German road map. I couldn't read German, but I identified a crossroad on there."

"I registered my battalion's fire on the crossroad, and then I shifted fire from there to any other target I wanted to hit."

"But I remember thinking when I was up there in the plane that Patton must be crazier than a loon, because he wouldn't slow down for Montgomery or anybody else. He wanted to get to Paris first."

When Georgie's column finally came to halt, it wasn't because of German resistance or delaying tactics; it was due to a lack of gasoline; Patton's tanks had run out of fuel.

At this stage of the European campaign, the majority of the supplies that were required to keep the Allied advance moving were being unloaded onto the beaches in Normandy. From there everything had to be moved inland to supply dumps and depots, and then trucked out to the point of the Allied advance.

24 hours a day, a never-ending stream of supply trucks drove back and forth between the front lines and the supply points far back in the rear. After a while, they couldn't keep up, and the gasoline quickly ran out.

"Patton had been up front with the tanks," Harold explains. "He came driving back along the road and was asking us to drain the gas from our fuel tanks so he could put it in the armor's tanks and continue on to Paris. He wasn't going to stop for anything. I thought he was nuts!"

"But then I realized that he knew more than I did about the current situation and the politics that were involved."

The lack of sufficient fuel did stop Patton, however; that, and the politics playing out among the Allies.

Charles de Gaulle, leader of the Free French, insisted that his men should be the first to enter the French capital city. To Patton's chagrin, the Allied command agreed. As a result, De Gaulle and his soldiers were the first liberators in the City of Light, with the Americans close behind.

When the joyous French soldiers entered their capital city on August 25, 1944, Harold and the men of the 202nd Field Artillery Battalion found themselves dug in on a tall hill just south of the city, providing fire support for the GI's of the 79th Infantry Division (ID) as they crossed the Seine River.

The crossing was proceeding well until the Germans launched a strong, concentrated counterattack with tanks and infantry. The Americans fought back and tried to hold onto their gains, but without enough men on the eastern side of the Seine, the oncoming enemy started to push the

GI's of the 79th ID back towards the river. Soon the call came in for artillery support.

Harold and the other observers quickly plotted coordinates on their maps, relaying the instructions to the batteries. The 12 howitzers of the Deuce opened up, sending the first of over 1,000 155mm shells into the attacking Germans. Smoke, flame and fountains of earth spewed into the air, quickly obscuring the view of the battlefield, but the howitzers continued to rain metal and high explosives down upon the Germans for nearly 30 minutes.

When the firing was complete and the smoke and dust subsided, the Germans had retreated with heavy losses, showing no signs of reorganizing for another attack.

With their momentum restored by the effectiveness of the Deuce's fire, the GI's of the 79th ID continued their push east, and more men and equipment poured over the Seine.

With the immediate threat neutralized, Harold and his driver then went out to scout, and in doing so, they were among those first GI's who drove in to Paris shortly after it's liberation.

"As the officer in charge of finding the best route of travel for the battalion, I had some freedom as far as scouting was concerned," Harold recalls. "My driver and I went into Paris soon after it fell."

"We hadn't ventured very far into the city when we were approached by a Frenchman who insisted on showing us the sights. We figured, why not? As long as we're here we might as well make the most of it."

"We spent a few hours with him as he took us down the Champs-Elysées to places like the Notre Dame Cathedral and the Eiffel Tower, all the while passing tanks along the way that were still burning from the recent fighting."

★ ★ ★

After the brief detour through Paris, Harold and his driver returned to the battalion. Heavy combat continued outside of the city, but beyond the range of the battalion's weapons. As a result, the Deuce moved out to get closer to the action; orders were issued to proceed to the small town of Pecy, 35 miles southeast of the outskirts of Paris.

Once in position in Pecy, the Deuce's howitzers undertook daily fire missions, the purpose of which was to harass the enemy and to prevent any German counterattacks.

In this they succeeded, and the guns of the 202nd remained deployed in the town for over a week as the Allies consolidated their positions before continuing the push across eastern France and onwards to the German border.

After the frenetic advance of the past four weeks, the time in Pecy was a welcome change; the men could finally catch up on some sorely-needed sleep.

"You get pretty tired when you're fighting and on the go," Harold says. "We didn't get much sleep."

"We had the GI coffee to help us keep going; it went everywhere we went. It was strong, and it tasted good when you got a canteen cup full…"

Then, reflecting back 60 years, he adds with a smile, "Of course you had to be careful not to burn your lips because that steel canteen cup really carried the heat!"

Photograph by Third Signal Company.   Courtesy of dogfacesoldiers.org

Vast quantities of German wreckage along the roads of France were an impediment to the speed of the Allied advance. As a result, U.S. Army Engineers were kept busy with clearing the roads so two-way traffic could be established: men and equipment had to move forward, and fuel and supply trucks needed to travel back to supply dumps.

HOWITZERS, GRASSHOPPERS, AND THE HOLY RIGHT HAND

Harold Brown Collection

A cold-looking Corporal David Mudge, Harold Brown's jeep driver, and 1st Lieutenant Samuel Giannetto, Harold's Assistant S-2 (Intelligence Officer), pose for the camera in early 1945. Lieutenant Giannetto assisted Harold with mess duties during the Battalion's move to Ireland. Corporal Mudge would accompany Harold on a memorable visit to a certain house in Austria during the last days of the war. Over the hood of the jeep is one of the brightly colored identification panels that were supposed to make the GI's on the ground visible to the Allied attack aircraft that were often overhead during the drive across Europe. As Harold personally experienced at a French schoolhouse, the panels didn't always work as advertised.

Chapter 10

Communication SNAFU's

★ ★ ★ ★ ★ ★ ★ ★

Allied artillery was instrumental in the breakout from Normandy, the battle to reduce the pocket of resistance in the Falaise Gap, and the rapid fighting advance to Paris.

Equally important, however, were the devastating attacks wrought by aircraft of the U.S. Army Air Force.

To maximize the effectiveness of air support, as well as to minimize casualties to friendly forces on the ground, the GI's below needed to communicate with the pilots above.

Unfortunately, radio technology of the 1940's did not allow for easy communication between different branches of the armed forces. Messages were relayed back through various communication chains (referred to as "channels"), with the expectation that the intended recipient would

HOWITZERS, GRASSHOPPERS, AND THE HOLY RIGHT HAND

actually receive the message. Too often, however, the message arrived incomplete, late, or not at all.

Ungainly, unreliable communication procedures were yet another example of the inefficiency of large military organizations of the 1940's, and the American soldiers had a unique phrase for this type of organizational shortcoming: SNAFU, which was a GI acronym for **S**ituation **N**ormal **A**ll **F**ouled **U**p. SNAFU's could occur just about anywhere and with anything, and the GI's accepted them as a way of Army life. Such acceptance, however, did not preclude the soldier's right to gripe about them!

☆ ☆ ☆

Ground troops communicated most often via phones, accessing other units through the miles of wire laid by the men of the Signal Corps. These communications specialists, though perhaps not always at the extreme forward point of the advance, were nonetheless up with the frontline troops, and subjected to similar dangers.

Take for instance what happened to 1st Lieutenant John Flaherty of the Deuce's HQ Battery who worked with the Wire Section.

"Lieutenant Flaherty was laying wire from the batteries to the battalion CP so they could get the phones up and working," Harold relates. "All of a sudden a bullet found him; grazed his neck from side to side. Luckily it didn't penetrate, for if it had he would have been in trouble."

COMMUNICATION SNAFU'S

Photograph by Third Signal Company.   Courtesy of dogfacesoldiers.org

A U.S. 105mm howitzer position during the American advance in Fall 1944. At left in the photograph, two GI's are using the ubiquitous field telephones that allowed the gun batteries to communicate with HQ.

"As it was he went to the battalion aid station, got the wound cleaned up and bandaged, and later that day he was back with us laying more wire. He was lucky."

Forward units also employed portable radio sets, although the low-powered transmitters were limited in range, usually of one to five miles depending on terrain.

By comparison, while aloft in a Grasshopper, radio range was greatly increased, and Harold could quickly radio firing adjustments back to his battalion as both he and the ground unit were using compatible equipment that transmitted on the same frequencies.

When the need arose to contact a friendly Army Air Force (AAF) aircraft however, it usually involved forwarding a message to a relay point that had access to the AAF communications net, a process which was very cumbersome. Nor was it time-efficient, as the routing of a message through the proper channels resulted in a significant delay before the message arrived at the intended destination, a delay that can mean the difference between life and death for those on the front lines.

This communication problem was widespread throughout World War II, and Harold was but one of thousands who dealt with the frustrations imposed by it.

"There were a few spotter flights when we were attacked by German fighters," Harold relates. "Our airplane was an easy target as we were slow and unarmed, so they never hesitated coming after us."

"I was busy scanning the ground with my field glasses looking for targets, and the pilot was intent on flying the pattern, but it was his responsibility to keep an eye out for flak and enemy fighters."

What would he and the pilot do if they were spotted by an enemy fighter?

"If we didn't spot the enemy plane before he attacked," explains Harold, "we wouldn't know we were in any danger until tracers started zipping past our wings!"

Even though the skies of France were dominated by the Allies, the Luftwaffe still sent occasional flights over the front line, searching for targets of opportunity. And a lone, slow-flying, unarmed Grasshopper definitely fit the target description.

Certainly there were Allied aircraft nearby, but the communication issues all but prevented a quick response to a call for help. As a result, the Grasshopper and its occupants often had to fend for themselves.

Surprisingly though, it was the slow speed of the spotter plane that saved Harold and his pilot.

"When we were attacked, the pilot would yank the stick to the side, and we would turn and dive quickly for the trees," he explains.

"We could turn more sharply since we were moving so slow. The German was traveling over 200 mph faster than our airplane, so he would be far past us before he could turn around, and his turn took him way out and around. Therefore usually they left us alone after the first pass."

HOWITZERS, GRASSHOPPERS, AND THE HOLY RIGHT HAND

★ ★ ★

Communications issues affected not just run-ins with the enemy, but encounters with friendly forces, too.

A frustrating event Harold witnessed that may have been caused by communication problems involved a damaged U.S. aircraft.

"There was a shot-up B-17 that was flying low near us, and he just kept circling, he was losing altitude," Harold remembers. "I called it in over the phone; we were trying to get him to crash on our side of the line. But apparently they couldn't contact him or he couldn't respond to any instructions."

"The plane got lower and lower and it disappeared behind a hill beyond us. Then we heard this big 'boom' as it hit the ground and burned up."

Harold and the men with him wished that they had been able to assist the pilot of the doomed aircraft, but they were relieved to know that some of the other men aboard had survived.

As Harold watched the big bomber slowly spiral down, some of the men were able to exit the aircraft.

"The crew bailed out," he says. "I stood there and watched those guys come down in their parachutes."

They didn't land anywhere nearby, so Harold never did find out any further details about the B-17 or the crew. The event was just another episode in the life and death struggle witnessed daily by the American soldiers fighting in World War II.

★ ★ ★

As it was, the sight of a B-17 was a very infrequent occurrence for the men of the 202nd Field Artillery Battalion as the big four-engine bombers usually flew at an altitude of 25,000 feet or higher on their way to targets in eastern France and Germany.

The aircraft that frontline GI's usually did see were the single-engine fighter-bombers that flew "down on the deck" in support of the ground troops.

With these heavily-armed aircraft in such close proximity to friendly troops, it was imperative that there be a clear, effective means of identifying Allied ground forces to prevent any attacks upon them by their own planes. Harold describes the method employed by the U.S. forces in Europe.

"We had fluorescent-type orange panels that we would drape over the hoods of the jeeps and other vehicles" he relates. "They were tied on there, and they were supposed to make us visible to our planes overhead."

When the battalion was not on the move, the panels were laid out on the ground in front of their positions.

"I don't know if they were effective or not," Harold states.

When asked to explain further, Harold elaborates, "We were at a schoolhouse building, in what town I don't remember, but a friendly fighter plane dove down and started to strafe us."

"I was inside when the bullets started hitting the building. I immediately backed up against the solid stone wall in between the sets of windows...it was maybe three feet wide."

"The bullets came into the building, broke all the windows, and shattered the furniture in the room, but I didn't get hurt...another lucky break."

"You had to think about those things ahead of time," he explains, "what you are going to do if something happens. The only thing you can do is hunt for the best cover you can find."

Good advice it seems, whether ducking German 88's in a hedgerow in Normandy, or avoiding U.S. Army Air Force .50 caliber slugs in a stone schoolhouse in central France.

COMMUNICATION SNAFU'S

Photograph by Third Signal Company.   Courtesy of dogfacesoldiers.org

The destructive waste of war is evidenced in yet another French town.

HOWITZERS, GRASSHOPPERS, AND THE HOLY RIGHT HAND

Photograph by Third Signal Company.   Courtesy of dogfacesoldiers.org

The French town of Brouvelieures is located in the vicinity of Charmes, and is surrounded by the wooded hills that are representative of the topography in this area of western France. In September 1944, Harold Brown had a dangerous encounter on one of the hills outside of Charmes.

Chapter 11

September 12, 1944

★ ★ ★ ★ ★ ★ ★ ★

As their second month in combat drew to a close, the men of the 202nd Field Artillery Battalion used a brief lull between actions to spend some time servicing their howitzers and vehicles. The rapid advance towards Paris had prevented performing major maintenance of any type, so the GI's of the Deuce serviced their equipment as best and as thoroughly as possible prior to the next order to move out.

That order came quickly on September 7, 1944, and the Deuce once again joined the U.S. Third Army's push to the east.

★ ★ ★

The advance was another rapid movement, with Patton exhorting his men to keep fighting, keep moving,

HOWITZERS, GRASSHOPPERS, AND THE HOLY RIGHT HAND

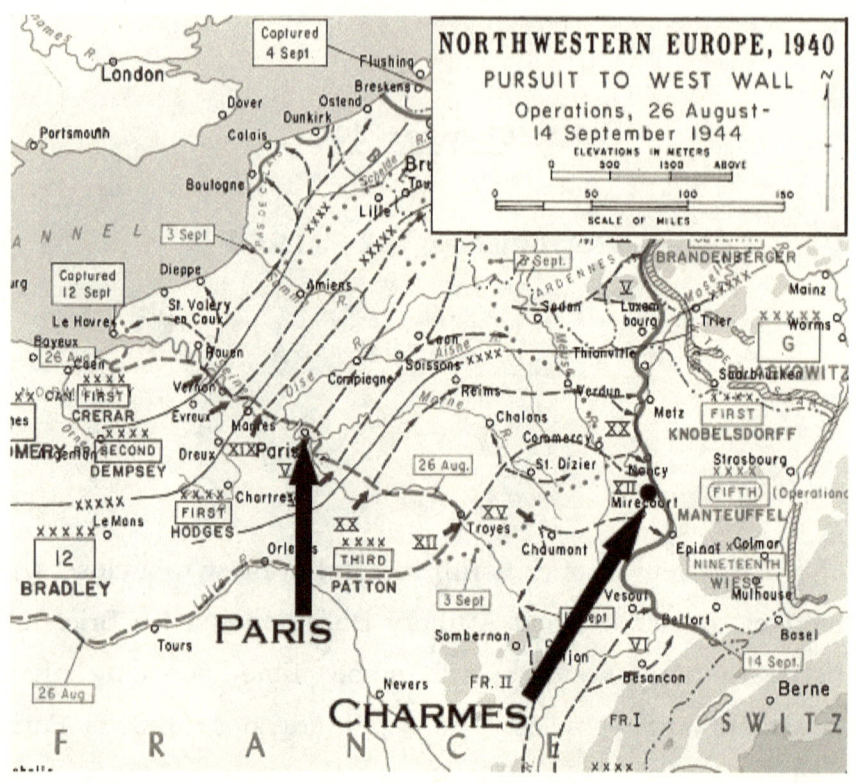

United States Army

As notated by the solid dark-gray line on the map, Harold Brown's mission of September 12, 1944, took him and his scouting party to the main line of German resistance south of Nancy, France.

keep pressuring the retreating Germans.

The 202nd FA Bn traveled 180 miles in 5 days, and September 12, 1944, found Harold out on a scouting mission in the hills 25 miles south of the German-held town of Nancy.

Harold's objective was to locate a good spotting location outside of the town of Charmes, and one hill in particular promised to be a good observation position as it overlooked the terrain down below.

Unfortunately, the hill would also turn out to be deadly.

Harold was traveling by jeep, and he and the men with him had just driven through Charmes on their way to the hills outside of town.

"The people in the town were leaning out of their windows, waving the white flags, celebrating because we were there," he remembers. "It was a good feeling."

Harold and his men didn't stop in Charmes, but proceeded through the town and into the hills beyond.

Without too much difficulty, Harold located one dominant hill that appeared to be well-suited as an observation position, and the artillerymen headed for it.

The scouting party parked their two jeeps at the base of the hill, and Harold took a look around for the best route up.

With him were three other GI's from the Deuce: 1st Lieutenant Gurden Flagg, Corporal Martin Johanson and Corporal Hoyt McAnally. All four men dismounted from the jeeps and began to trudge up the steep hillside which was crossed by contour depressions, shallow furrows running horizontally across the hillside.

They were steadily making their way up the hill when the afternoon silence of the French countryside was abruptly shattered.

"It was September 12, 1944," Harold says resolutely. "We were walking along the hillside when all of a sudden a machine gun starts chattering, and the bullets started hitting at our feet, in the side of the hill."

"Those German MG-34's had a high rate of fire, higher than our machine guns...bullets were flying all over the place."

All four men hit the ground, looking desperately for a depression or rock that would get them out of the sites of the German gun.

"We all started crawling, looking for some shelter," Harold continues. "From where I was, the contours offered the only cover from the machine gun fire, so I got into one immediately."

"At first we couldn't see where the fire was coming from. There was a clearing at the base of the hill, maybe 100 to 200 yards wide, with thick trees on the other side. In the

SEPTEMBER 12, 1944

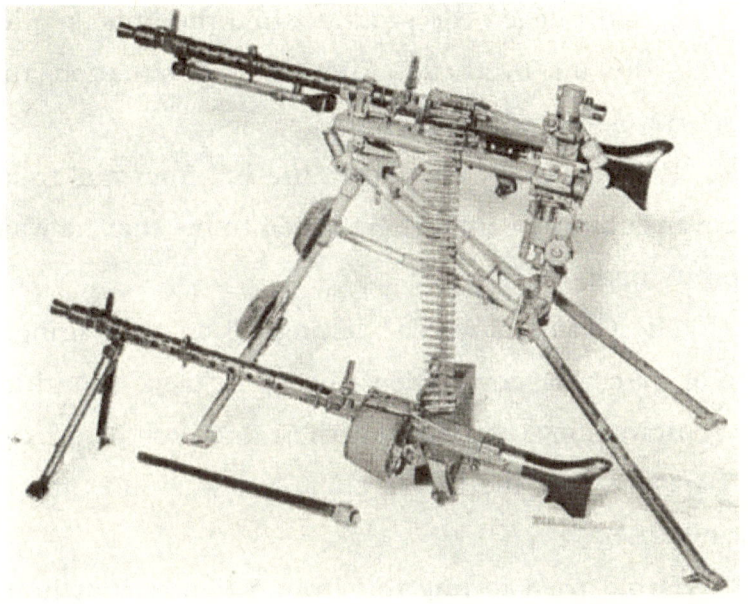

United States Army

The German MG-34 machine gun was a reliable, well-made weapon that featured a very high rate of fire. This was probably the type of weapon that fired upon Harold and his scouting party on the hillside outside of Charmes, France.

initial confusion it was hard to pinpoint the location of the German gun."

Harold hugged the ground while the bullets snapped through the air overhead. Then a bad situation turned worse: Harold heard cries for help.

"Hoyt McAnally was down the hill from me, trying to get cover behind a contour. He yelled to me that he was hit, hit pretty bad."

"The Germans weren't letting up on their firing, and none of us could move. Then I heard a "plop" sound in the dirt contour above my helmet, then another "plop." One of the Germans had me in his sites and was shooting at me with his rifle."

Harold tried to hug the ground tighter, but he knew he had to get to better cover.

"I just couldn't stick my head up long enough to find a place to go to," he says.

With the Germans firing steadily, neither he, Flagg nor Johanson could get to the wounded McAnally, and they were too far from their jeeps and the shelter the vehicles would provide.

"It's really frustrating," Harold explains. "You have someone who needs your help, but you aren't able to get to them. When any of us tried to move, the Germans instantly targeted us with their fire. It's *real* frustrating." Yet Harold realized that he couldn't stay a target for long.

"With the German rifle bullets striking the ground near my head, I finally decided to make a run for better cover. It was an awful feeling having bullets hitting near my face...I can't describe to you what it felt like."

"However, I finally decided I had to do something, so I jumped up and ran across the hillside to a deeper depression, which I made it to OK."

Though Harold did survive the war without any serious wounds, he was bloodied on this day.

"The ground was rocky all along the hillside," he explains, "so when the machine gun bullets hit, little rock splinters went everywhere. I was hit repeatedly in the face and hands, anywhere where my skin wasn't protected. Luckily, the Germans weren't able to directly hit me."

Gurden Flagg also decided it was time to make a move to better cover.

"Lieutenant Flagg was crawling on his belly, squeezing under a fence when the German machine gun targeted him," Harold recalls. "Most of the bullets hit the earth in front of him or passed over him."

"But one of the bullets grazed his back; burned a crease into his skin from one side of his back to the other. If it had been an inch lower, it would have torn into him and hit his spine. He was lucky."

With the German gunners concentrating on the struggling Lieutenant Flagg, another of the pinned-down GI's decided to make a move.

"Martin Johanson was a big guy, a veteran of the Swedish Army," Harold relates. "And he was an expert with the M1. He always carried his rifle with him, and luckily he didn't leave it in the jeep on this day."

"By this time he had sited the German machine gun in the trees across the clearing from the base of the hill. He just needed to get to a position where he could take them under fire."

"Johanson was able to work his way behind a small rock that offered some cover, and from there he got the Germans in his sites. He opened fire with his M1 and quickly ran the riflemen off, and then continuing his fire he forced back the machine gun crew too."

As the Germans withdrew, with Johanson and his M1 ready to provide covering fire, Harold and Gurden Flagg were finally able to go to the aid of Hoyt McAnally.

Sadly, there wasn't a lot they could do.

"He was hit in the groin," Harold says. "The bullet had severed the artery in his leg...we couldn't stop the bleeding."

After gingerly placing Hoyt in the back of one of the jeeps and making him as comfortable as possible, Harold, Gurden and Martin quickly drove back to U.S. lines.

By the time they reached the aid station however, it was too late. Corporal Hoyt McAnally had died on the way, becoming one of the 12 men of the Deuce, and one of the

SEPTEMBER 12, 1944

405,000 Americans, who made the ultimate sacrifice in World War II.

★ ★ ★

"Yep, that was a close one...I thought about that day for many years," Harold says.

"I wondered what I could have done differently. I kept thinking that if I had taken us around the other side of the hill, maybe Hoyt McAnally would still be alive."

"But then I thought that based on where the German machine gun was located, if I had gone around the other side of the hill we all might have been killed...it's hard to say."

Harold pauses briefly, then, with the painful memory evident in the expression on his face, he says, "You always wonder if there was something else you could have done."

U.S. Army Signal Corps

A U.S. Army halftrack slogs its way through a quagmire of mud, while in the background, GI's struggle to free stuck vehicles.

Chapter 12

Mud, Snow...and the Bulge

★ ★ ★ ★ ★ ★ ★ ★

The end of September 1944 ushered in two major changes for Harold and the 202nd Field Artillery Battalion: the French rainy season had arrived, and on September 29, 1944, the battalion was put under the direction of Lieutenant General Alexander M. Patch and his U.S. Seventh Army.

The rain fell steadily nearly every day, and the wet weather turned the French dirt roads and fields into quagmires which would swallow a howitzer up to it's axles in no time. Every movement and deployment undertaken by the Battalion was a difficult struggle against the thick, sticky, boot-sucking mud. Vehicle winches were in near-constant use, pulling stuck howitzers, jeeps and trucks from the mud. Observation flights were impossible as even the

U.S. Army Signal Corps

A river of mud for a roadway in Europe during late Fall 1944.

light-weight Grasshoppers couldn't safely take-off or land in the muck, and the men cut down many a French tree for use as a corduroy road surface.

Fire missions against the Germans were plentiful, though, and in the deep mud the recoil from each round would push the gun trails deeper and deeper into the muck, resulting in much cussing and sweating from the cannoneers as they struggled to free the howitzers when the next order came to move out.

"The mud over there was unbelievable," Harold remembers. "We had to put two of our tracked prime movers on a gun just to free it from the stuff."

The going was now very slow, and it was safe to say that the race across France had ended.

As Patton's U.S. Third Army headed northeast towards its eventual assault on central Germany, the 202nd Field Artillery Battalion was attached to General Patch's forces coming up from the south of France, with southern Germany and Austria as the U.S. Seventh Army's goal.

Before the border of Germany could be crossed, however, there remained the task of pushing the Germans from the Vosges Mountains in eastern France, a job that would not be easy due to the onset of the rains, and the hardships of winter following close behind.

Photograph by Third Signal Company.   Courtesy of dogfacesoldiers.org

The Alsace plain in France, with the Vosges Mountains rising in the distance.

Photograph by Third Signal Company.   Courtesy of dogfacesoldiers.org

Lieutenant General Alexander Patch,
U.S. Seventh Army commander.
(2nd from left)

Photograph by Third Signal Company. Courtesy of dogfacesoldiers.org

U.S. M8 Scout Cars were often employed at the front of the advance for reconnaissance. As such, they were prone to being targets of attacks by German main line or rear guard units. Harold Brown did all of his ground-based scouting in a jeep or on foot, both methods which made him a smaller target for enemy fire.

Photograph by Third Signal Company.   Courtesy of dogfacesoldiers.org

Of course, many German scout cars met the same fate as the American one on the preceding page.

HOWITZERS, GRASSHOPPERS, AND THE HOLY RIGHT HAND

October 1944 passed nondescriptly, with day after day of mud, difficult movement and the steady firing of 155mm shells onto German positions.

By the first week of November 1944, the rain had turned to snow, and now the bone-chilling cold of winter was added to the discomforts endured by the American GI's on the front lines in France.

The pace of the Allied advance had slowed considerably as the Deuce had advanced but 25 miles since mid-September. They had passed through the town of Lunèville southeast of Nancy, then east to Mènil-Flin. From there the howitzers of the 202nd Field Artillery Battalion would support the drive to take the Saverne Gap in the Vosges Mountains which rise up from the plain of Alsace. Once the Gap was secure, Patch could move his forces through it and toward the city of Strasbourg...and just beyond the city limits lay the swift-flowing waters of the Rhine River.

Harold's recollections of this particular time on the front line are mainly those of days that blur together, with one particular exception.

"We weren't moving very far during late-1944," he says. "The weather was terrible, but the batteries still fired daily at targets, and there were still quite a few scouting missions as we always had to keep tabs on what the Germans were up to."

MUD, SNOW...AND THE BULGE

Photograph by Third Signal Company.   Courtesy of dogfacesoldiers.org

American vehicles move into the town of Clairefontaine, passing over bridges erected by U.S. Army Engineers. From Charmes, the Deuce traveled through Clairefontaine, which is located at the foot of the Vosges Mountains in western France.

Photograph by Third Signal Company. Courtesy of dogfacesoldiers.org

A U.S. 155mm howitzer, pulled by its tracked prime mover, makes its way over a Bailey bridge through the soggy French weather that was so prevalent in Fall of 1944.

MUD, SNOW...AND THE BULGE

"With the weather as bad as it was," he remembers, "most of our scouting missions were done on the ground."

It was during one of these scouting missions that Harold recalls an event that now, 63 years later, seems almost humorous to him.

"I was out in the countryside poking around," he relates, "when right in front of me, about 40 yards away, this German soldier pops up out of the bushes and starts running. He startled me, but I pulled out my .45 and started to strafe him."

"Now, the pistol is only accurate to about 25 yards, so against a moving target it's practically useless, but I fired it anyway. Boy, you should have seen him move when I started firing! He was wearing one of those long, gray overcoats and the coattails were just *flying* in the air as he ran away from me."

"He was running as hard as he could go, and there I was standing with my pistol trying to hit him, and of course I didn't hit him at all!"

"After it was over, all I could think about was him in that huge coat, running like crazy with the coattails flapping along behind him! To this day I get a smile thinking about the whole scene, and part of me wishes I could track him down and ask him if he remembers."

It seems that Harold was lucky yet again, for the hidden German saw Harold coming, but Harold didn't see him until the German started running.

"Now that I think about it," Harold says, "he didn't appear to be carrying a rifle; maybe he only had a sidearm like me. I don't know what he was doing there other than hiding from us. Maybe he was an observer, or maybe he was just relieving himself...who knows?"

"If he was armed, he certainly could have had a good shot at me."

★ ★ ★

General Patch's drive to take the Saverne Gap kicked-off on November 12, 1944. The guns of the 202nd Field Artillery Battalion were busy once again, firing in support of the GI's of the 79th Infantry Division.

As the foot soldiers advanced, the men of the Deuce would move up too, deploying the howitzers 3000 to 5000 yards behind the front line. This process was repeated over and over, day after day.

When weather permitted, the Grasshoppers took to the air with an observer aboard, providing the accurate fire adjustments that such flights made possible. As the men of the Deuce would see, however, the dangers of such flights were not strictly limited to enemy fire.

"We had a replacement, a new liaison pilot named Lieutenant Orris Herr," Harold recalls. "He was up in a spotter plane in mid-November with the pilot, Lieutenant

John White, and they were directing fire when all of a sudden the aircraft exploded."

"Apparently they were hit by one of our shells - just an accident - as they were in the same spot of air where that shell was traveling through. What are the chances of that happening?"

Incredibly enough, it was a scene that was unfortunately repeated again that same month. Another new observer, Lieutenant George Schleier, and pilot, Lieutenant Allen Hathaway, were killed when their Grasshopper was also hit in mid-air by a friendly artillery round.

"We went to the crash sites, and there wasn't much left," Harold says. "Those airplanes are just fabric and metal frame, so there was nothing left. We picked up what body parts we could find…it wasn't a pretty scene."

As Harold experienced throughout the war, to keep one's sanity and effectiveness as a soldier, events such as what had happened to the two spotter flights had to be pushed to the back of the mind, and the focus had to remain on the job at hand: defeating the Germans.

★   ★   ★

The U.S. Seventh Army's drive into the Vosges Mountains was a slow one, and Thanksgiving Day 1944 found Harold and the Deuce deployed near the small French town of Brouviller.

Harold Brown Collection

Forward Observer 2nd Lieutenant Shelton Greenberg, sporting a shearling and leather flight jacket, replaced 1st Lieutenant John White who was killed by friendly fire while on an artillery spotting flight in 1944.

Brouviller was only 15 miles west of the Saverne Gap, the strategic passage through the mountains.

The battle for the Gap was in its final stage, with the 202nd Field Artillery Battalion's howitzers doing their part by firing in support of the GI's of the 44th Infantry Division. The big guns of the Deuce were targeting a German panzer division that was attempting to outflank the 44th ID, and the situation was tense. The Battalion Mess personnel, however, hoped to provide a little relief to the artillerymen manning the guns.

As a break from the daily rigors of combat, the U.S. Army high command had decided that on this day, all GI's were to receive a warm, proper Thanksgiving meal, if at all possible.

Due to the serious threat posed by the German attack, however, the Deuce's turkey dinner was delayed numerous times as the American artillery was called into action repeatedly throughout the evening of November 25th. Eventually though, with the arrival of nightfall, Harold and his fellow artillerymen were finally able to eat their meal and grab a little rest.

"We ate our turkey dinner out of our mess kits," he remembers. "Not very fancy, but it was a nice change from the K and C Rations we normally ate."

The break was short-lived, however, as dawn of November 26th brought a renewal of combat, and the howitzers were once again back in action.

HOWITZERS, GRASSHOPPERS, AND THE HOLY RIGHT HAND

Photograph by Third Signal Company. Courtesy of dogfacesoldiers.org

A GI examines the bodies of German soldiers who were killed during the drive to the Saverne Gap in November 1944. Abandoned MG-34's lay on the ground alongside the fence in the left of the photograph.

Photograph by Third Signal Company.   Courtesy of dogfacesoldiers.org

Another dead German soldier testifies to the hurried Wehrmacht withdrawal during the Saverne Gap action. At least 15 GI's are visible riding on the M-10 Tank Destroyer as it passes the fallen enemy.

Photograph courtesy of Rich Heller   warfoto.com

A 155mm Howitzer M1 in full-recoil during action in the French Vosges Mountains, November 1944.

Thanks to determined American resistance, the tactical situation for the 44th Infantry Division improved throughout the morning, and the German armor was finally forced to withdraw. This change of circumstance, however, did not mean the men of the Deuce could now sit back and relax.

New orders were issued, the battalion made ready to redeploy, and the night of November 26, 1944, found the 202nd Field Artillery Battalion rolling through the Gap itself, up the Saverne Pass to the French town of Mommenheim.

The Deuce deployed its howitzers in a clearing outside of Mommenheim, and the fighting briefly quieted down as the Americans brought more men through the Saverne Gap and consolidated their forces.

Within a couple of days when sufficient strength had been brought forward, the GI's resumed the push west, and on November 30, 1944, the Deuce moved to the northwest, 20 miles from the French town of Rimling.

Harold and his men were now less than 40 miles from the German border.

✯ ✯ ✯

HOWITZERS, GRASSHOPPERS, AND THE HOLY RIGHT HAND

Photograph by Third Signal Company.   Courtesy of dogfacesoldiers.org

After taking the Saverne Gap, the U.S. Seventh Army moved on Strasbourg, France, in preparation for the assault on the German border. Extreme supply shortages, however, would delay the offensive until Spring of 1945. In the photograph above, U.S. Sherman tanks roll into Strasbourg.

MUD, SNOW...AND THE BULGE

As December 1, 1944, dawned, the Deuce was assigned the task of providing artillery fire in support of GI's of the 87th Infantry Division as they attempted to clear the fortifications of the German-occupied Maginot Line.

For the first two weeks of December, the howitzers of the 202nd Field Artillery Battalion fired on the concrete forts and pillboxes that the French had built in the 1930's to protect their country from another German invasion.

"I had three forward observers out with the infantry during the attacks on the Maginot Line," Harold relates. "When a target would pop up, they'd call in a fire mission, and we'd pelt those domes and pillboxes that were protruding above the ground, though I don't know what effect it had."

The 155mm shells indeed had little impact on the reinforced concrete emplacements, but they were very effective at keeping the Wehrmacht troops inside the Line's fortifications and tunnels. The advancing GI's of the 87th ID were therefore able to successfully attack the Maginot defenses, and route the Germans from their sheltered positions.

After the tunnels were cleared, Harold had a chance to tour the Maginot Line.

"The tunnels were full of equipment the Germans had left behind," he recalls. "Tunnel after tunnel after tunnel."

Photograph by Third Signal Company. Courtesy of dogfacesoldiers.org

Armed with an M1 rifle and a .30 caliber air-cooled machine gun, a GI covers a section of the German-occupied Maginot Line in eastern France.

A HEAVY FORT ON THE MAGINOT LINE NEAR RIMLING. "A" BATTERY'S OP WAS IN THIS FORT FOR A TIME.

202nd Field Artillery Battalion Unit History

A disabled German Panther tank sits outside of a concrete emplacement on the Maginot Line. Harold Brown examined this fort and the extensive tunnels that were connected to it.

Harold Brown Collection

This French family kindly offered their house to Harold Brown and other men of the Deuce for a few nights during the fighting along the Maginot Line in December 1944.

"Occasionally there would be one of those domes with a cannon or machine gun mounted in it, and maybe a few rifle slits," Harold explains.

"I remember thinking at the time, 'What the heck good is the Maginot Line? It's mostly underground!' I couldn't see any sense in the Germans putting all those men in the tunnels, men who couldn't fight back."

★   ★   ★

With the Maginot Line neutralized, the GI's pushed steadily beyond it, closing in on the German frontier. Fire missions in support of the advancing American infantry were continued by the Deuce until the third week of December 1944. Around that time some news began filtering through of a German counterattack in the Ardennes Forest in Belgium, but that was over 130 miles to the north of the Deuce.

Initially the beginnings of the massive action that would be called the Battle of the Bulge did not greatly concern those GI's who were on the line far to the south... they had their own war to fight.

"We were keeping an eye on what was happening up there," Harold says, 'but we were occupied with our own section of the front."

On December 21st, the Deuce moved 20 miles east to the town of Rimling. They were now less than two miles from the German border, and from Rimling some of the forward observers actually crossed over into Germany. This "invasion" of German soil was not to last, however, as the events unfolding in Belgium were now affecting units deployed around the Deuce.

The Germans had achieved a major breakthrough, and the Allied high command was scrambling to shift forces to meet the threat.

Of the three infantry divisions assigned to the Deuce's sector, two were pulled from the line and sent north to help stem the German advance in the Ardennes. The remaining infantry division, the 100th, now had to cover a section of the front line that was normally held by three divisions, a situation which greatly benefited the Germans as they could easily slip patrols through the U.S. line.

Soon the patrols gave way to larger German attacks, and without enough frontline soldiers to effectively hold the line, the U.S. Seventh Army needed to fall back to a better defensive location. Consequently, Harold was instructed to look for a position to the rear of the battalion's current location.

"As I was always out in front of the battalion, I would make a note of any areas we passed that looked suitable for the batteries to be deployed in," he explains. "There were many locations you couldn't place the guns in as you needed to have an open area without any obstructions; trees were always a problem."

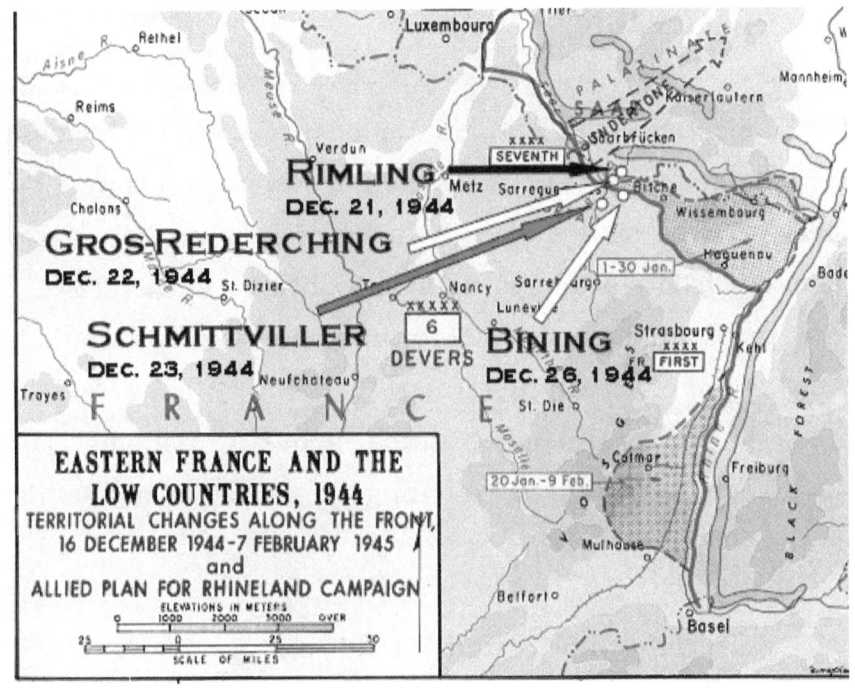

United States Army

The back-and-forth maneuverings of the Deuce to the west of Bitche, France, in late-December 1944. Needless to say, Harold Brown and his fellow artillerymen weren't able to take part in much Christmas celebrating that year.

"If I passed an area I thought would be suitable, I'd make a note of the coordinates so I could quickly find the location if needed."

On December 22nd, the Deuce moved back three miles to the small town of Gros-Rèderching, then the following day back another six miles to the town of Schmittviller. Harold and his fellow artillerymen spent Christmas Day 1944 in that tiny French town, not knowing if the Battalion would be staying put or retreating further,

"I don't remember much about Christmas Day," Harold states. "I was out scouting...just another normal day for us."

December 26th found Harold and the Deuce moving once again, this time forward five miles to Bining. This move, like all, required great physical effort of the men as old positions had to be dismantled and the new positions had to be established. Ground had to be cleared, aiming circles and stakes placed in the snow at the correct spots, and ammunition brought in to the gun positions.

These near-constant moves in the snow and ice of late-December 1944 were exhausting, and did not leave the men in much of a mood for holiday celebrating. There were simply too many day-to-day unknowns for any of them to be able to focus on what the future year might hold.

Compounding their feelings of weariness, the GI's of the Deuce were retreating for the first time, and this had a disheartening effect on the Battalion's morale. Ever since they had come ashore in Normandy the direction of travel had been forward, and the men and their psyches had become accustomed to the success.

☆ ☆ ☆

Thus, as 1944 drew to a close, Harold and the men of the 202nd Field Artillery Battalion found themselves very tired and cold, and faced by what seemed to be a resurgent German Army.

With the New Year approaching, their situation was about to take another turn for the worse.

HOWITZERS, GRASSHOPPERS, AND THE HOLY RIGHT HAND

National Archives

American GI's of the 100th Infantry Division man a makeshift defensive position in the Vosges Mountains during December 1944. Soon they would have their hands full with the German NORDWIND offensive.

Chapter 13

NORDWIND

☆ ☆ ☆ ☆ ☆ ☆ ☆ ☆

On New Year's Eve 1944, with his Ardennes offensive stalled, Adolf Hitler decided to initiate another attempt to turn the tide on the western front: Operation NORDWIND.

Hitler's objective was the strategic Saverne Gap, and Patch's U.S. Seventh Army, including Harold Brown and the 202nd Field Artillery Battalion, was in the way.

☆ ☆ ☆

German military intelligence knew the line in front of the Deuce was thinly held as a result of the shift of American divisions to the Ardennes, but Allied intelligence had been able to determine that the Germans were planning an offensive there. With this knowledge, the late-December withdrawals undertaken by the Deuce were part of the Allied

HOWITZERS, GRASSHOPPERS, AND THE HOLY RIGHT HAND

plan to defend against this German attack into the Alsace region of France.

The U.S. Seventh Army had consolidated its lines which, though weakly defended, were manned by GI's who were expecting an attack. Unlike the GI's in the Ardennes who were taken completely by surprise when the Germans struck, Patch's troops were dug in and alert, ready to meet the attack which was expected to commence on New Year's Day 1945.

Hitler, however, did not plan on waiting until the new year to send his forces forward.

Late in the evening on Dec. 31, 1944, troopers of the 17th SS Panzergrenadier Division and 36th Volksgrenadier Division hit the GI's of the U.S. 44th and 100th Infantry Divisions on the line just east of Rimling.

The SS divisions were among Hitler's most feared, and were composed of fanatical Nazi's, whereas the Volks or "peoples" soldiers were a cobbled-together collection of regular army transferees, young boys, old men, and others who were initially considered to be unsuitable for combat service.

Together, the two German divisions commenced the attack on New Years Eve, and pressed forward against the waiting Americans.

★   ★   ★

Photograph by Third Signal Company.   Courtesy of dogfacesoldiers.org

A U.S. M10 Tank Destroyer on the line in eastern France during Winter of 1944/45.

HOWITZERS, GRASSHOPPERS, AND THE HOLY RIGHT HAND

Photograph by Third Signal Company.   Courtesy of dogfacesoldiers.org

American medics evacuate a wounded GI from the front lines in January 1945. The early-war development of dried blood plasma saved the lives of countless U.S. servicemen during World War II. Stored in two metal cans (one containing the dried plasma, the other water for reconstitution), dried plasma was easy to transport, and unlike whole blood, did not require refrigeration. If a wounded GI survived long enough to make it to an aid station or field hospital, his chances of survival were very high. Many times, a wounded individual made it that far due to medics administering dried blood plasma.

NORDWIND

In the waning hours of December 31, 1944, fierce fighting erupted all along the American line in front of the Deuce, and the howitzers of the 202nd Field Artillery Battalion rang-in the New Year by opening fire on the German soldiers and panzers who were leading the attack five miles from the batteries' positions.

The Germans made slow but steady progress, and by the afternoon of January 1, 1945, enemy troops were just outside of the town of Gros-Rederching, three miles from the Deuce.

With the Germans on the offensive and out in the open, targets for the howitzers were plentiful. Harold and the other observers called in a continuous stream of fire coordinates, and the battalion's 155mm shells pounded the German advance throughout the day. Mixed in with the shells of high-explosives were rounds with proximity fuzes, the dreaded "airburst" shells that were so feared by soldiers on the ground.

Instead of exploding upon contact with the ground where most of the explosive energy and shrapnel was directed, proximity-fuzed shells would explode in the air, spraying their deadly shrapnel downward over a wide area.

"These shells were top-secret up until that time in the war," Harold explains. "We could set the fuze to explode a certain distance above the ground, usually 20 yards up. The nose of the shell had a miniature radio transmitter inside that would sense when the shell was at the right height, then it would explode, sending the shrapnel spraying out over a wide area."

"The Germans were terrified of the things. When we started to take prisoners, the POW's would ask us about our 'secret weapon' that we had been firing at them."

The airburst shells were very effective against targets out in the open, and certainly took a toll among the advancing German grenadiers. But onward the Germans came, slowly pushing back the stubbornly resisting GI's of the 44th and 100th Infantry Divisions.

As the attack continued, the Germans were able to move their own artillery forward, and the 202nd Field Artillery Battalion soon started receiving heavy enemy counter fire. To avoid the incoming "mail", the Deuce's gun crews shifted their howitzers to other firing positions numerous times throughout the day.

During one of these moves on New Years Day, the men of the Deuce had an experience that was much too close for comfort.

"I remember New Years Day 1945 as clear as today," Harold explains. "The weather was terrible...cold and snow...and the Germans were advancing our way."

"Earlier in the day Colonel Lewis had called me over to the CP. He was always a man of few words, and he said, 'Brown, get some observers out there.' I told him I already had them out; we had been notified that the Germans were

Harold Brown Collection

Captain Harold Brown during Winter 1944/45.

going to hit us...but we *weren't* told they were going to break through!"

"Late that evening after dark we tried to fall back, but we couldn't get the howitzers out on the roads. The field we were in was a mess, and we couldn't tow the equipment to the roadway."

"Then all of a sudden we get a report that Germans are coming down the road towards us! We didn't have time to deploy the guns, and it was no time at all before we heard the approaching enemy column. I don't know how big it was, but they had a lot of vehicles with them, including tanks."

"We stayed back away from the road, drew our side arms and rifles, and listened as they passed us in the dark...it was quite an experience."

★   ★   ★

The large enemy patrol that passed the Deuce on New Years Day was just a precursor of what was to come. By the morning of January 3rd, the main body of the German attack was only 1 ½ miles from the Deuce's batteries. The 202nd Field Artillery Battalion was again ordered to fall back, and Harold scouted a safe route southwest, five miles to where the battalion had spent Christmas, at Schmittviller. From there, the Deuce hammered away at the Germans, the big guns firing nearly continuously.

"We were a little nervous in a situation like that," Harold recalls. "But we had a lot of firepower. Each howitzer

Photograph by Third Signal Company.   Courtesy of dogfacesoldiers.org

The Alsace town of Ostheim appears desolate and deserted, as did many French towns near the front lines in January 1945.

could fire 3 rounds a minute without overheating the tube (the howitzer gun barrel). That's 36 rounds a minute from the whole battalion. When all those rounds are targeted on one area, it makes for a pretty intense concentration of fire, one that could break up most attacks. We always felt confident we could put up a strong fight if we had to."

Then again, in the right circumstance, a single gun could also save the day.

"One of our batteries was approached by a German tank that had broken through," Harold relates. "The tank was so close that the four battery gunners could not site their howitzers on it, weren't able to use the aiming mechanism."

"1st Lieutenant Otis Oothoudt had the presence of mind to open the breach on one of the guns, and he directed the gun crew to move the aiming mechanism until he had the German tank visually sited through the bore of the howitzer. Then they loaded the weapon and fired on the German."

"Oothoudt repeated the aiming procedure again and again. Our 155mm shells couldn't penetrate the tank's armor, but you can bet the Germans inside got a good shaking every time one of the shells hit! They quickly decided that they had had enough, and took off out of there."

So when employed the correct way, a single howitzer that wasn't able to destroy German tanks could at least run one off.

"Lieutenant Oothoudt was awarded the Silver Star for that one," Harold says with a smile.

☆ ☆ ☆

In those first few days of 1945, the guns of the Deuce continued to relentlessly pound the enemy. Combined with the tough resistance put up by the American infantrymen on the ground, the German NORDWIND advance slowly ground to a halt. By January 5th the outcome was decided: NORDWIND, like Hitler's Ardennes gamble, was a failure.

For the next two weeks, the Germans attacked off and on, trying to breach the American defenses. But the GI's of the 44th and 100th Infantry Divisions were staying put; the line held. By January 17th, it appeared that the German advance was spent, and the front quieted down considerably.

☆ ☆ ☆

After more than two months of near-constant maneuvering and heavy firing, the men of the Deuce were exhausted, and ready for a breather.

The men's hopes for such a break would have to wait, however. Harold had just scouted a route to a new position, and the 202nd Field Artillery Battalion would be moving out the next day.

HOWITZERS, GRASSHOPPERS, AND THE HOLY RIGHT HAND

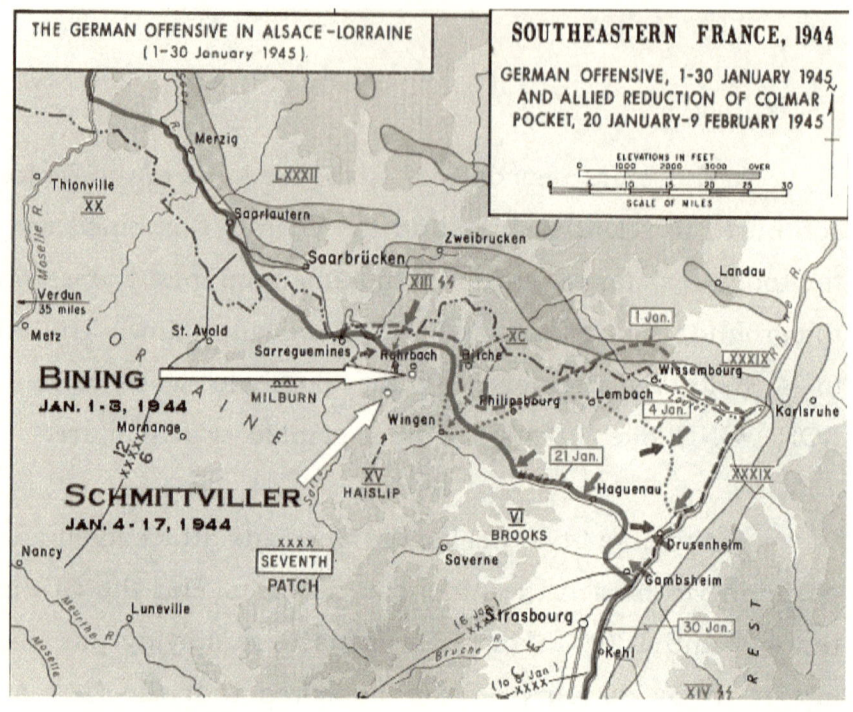

United States Army

The dashed line depicts the front line on January 1, 1945 as the Germans launched Operation NORDWIND, and the solid line depicts the extent of the enemy advance on January 21, 1945. Hitler's goal for NORDWIND was the strategic Saverne Gap, located in the lower center of the map, just to the right of the notation for General Patch's U.S. Seventh Army.

Harold Brown Collection

From the left, Lieutenants Marvin Krouse, Lester Uren, and Otis Othoudt during Winter 1944/45. Lieutenant Othoudt was awarded the Silver Star for the quick-thinking he exhibited when his battery was threatened by a German tank.

Photograph by Third Signal Company.   Courtesy of dogfacesoldiers.org

The Vosges Mountains in eastern France.

Chapter 14

Winter in the Vosges Mountains

★ ★ ★ ★ ★ ★ ★ ★

January 18, 1945, found the men and vehicles of the 202nd Field Artillery Battalion traveling the twisting, snow-covered roads of the Vosges Mountains in eastern France. Their destination was Guisberg, and, unbeknownst to them, the town would end up being their home for the next two months.

Winter had descended fully on this section of the European battlefront; conditions were bitter, the roads were icy and treacherous. Travel by foot was difficult, and travel by vehicle was hazardous. Now more than ever, the Americans in eastern France would be content to just stay put for a while. After the back and forth fighting that ushered in the new year, the GI's on the line were quite tired. Fortunately, the Germans had apparently exhausted themselves with the failed NORDWIND operation, and they, too, appeared to be content with laying low.

The Allied command would have preferred to keep the pressure on the Germans. The U.S. and British armies, however, could not take advantage of the depleted strength of the enemy.

After stemming the German advance in the Ardennes as well as the following attack in Alsace, supply shortages had reached the critical stage. Of the multitude of items required for an Allied push into Germany, there simply weren't enough quantities on hand to sustain a drive up to and over the Rhine River. The Allied command had a tough decision to make, but the supply problems made the answer clear. After conferring with his Corps commanders, General Eisenhower decided to delay any major operations while his armies stockpiled supplies for a spring offensive.

★ ★ ★

Harold recalls these early months of 1945 as a time of very cold winter weather, and of limited ammunition.

"When we got to Guisberg we established ourselves in an old farmhouse that wasn't too badly shot up," he says. "It was the middle of winter, so we were relieved to have cover over our heads. When we had chance to sleep we would lay our bedrolls down on the floor and get some rest," a comfort which was a welcome change from the hard ground and foxholes Harold and his fellow GI's had been sleeping in.

DEUCE-O-DEUCE CP AT GUISEBERG, FRANCE. AND WHAT DO YOU KNOW — MUD AND SNOW IN THE FOREGROUND!

202nd Field Artillery Battalion Unit History

The building occupied by Harold Brown and the 202nd Field Artillery Battalion's HQ during their stay at Guisberg (the caption states "Guiseberg", which is an incorrect spelling).

Photograph by Third Signal Company.   Courtesy of dogfacesoldiers.org

The wooded, rolling terrain of the Vosges Mountains. Once Hitler's NORDWIND offensive was halted in mid-January 1945, the emphasis for the GI's was on staying as warm and comfortable as possible throughout the remainder of the cold, snowy winter.

Photograph by Third Signal Company. Courtesy of dogfacesoldiers.org

"Luxury" shelters such as this one helped the artillerymen cope with the harsh winter weather in the Vosges Mountains.

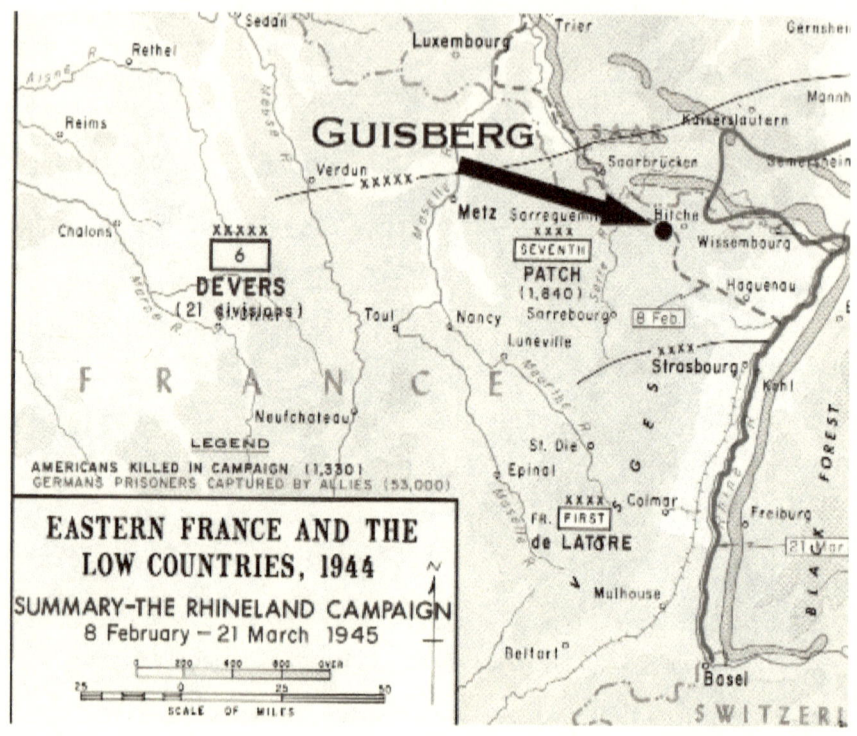

United States Army

The map clearly depicts Guisberg's location on the front line, as notated by the dashed line running roughly north-by-northwest. The gray-shaded areas to the east of the dashed line represent Germany's Westwall, the defensive fortifications which comprised the Siegfried Line. Assaulting the German defenses would be delayed until the arrival of favorable spring weather in March 1945.

"We were fairly comfortable in that spot," he states. "As it turned out, we stayed there for quite a while. The food supply was pretty good, and I had a pair of tanker pants with wool lining, and winter shoepacs to help me keep warm on my spotting missions."

"But we were instructed to conserve our ammunition, to fire only when necessary. The supply units were trying to stockpile ammunition for the planned spring offensive."

Nevertheless, the battalion still had a few fire missions each day, and the forward observers and Grasshopper pilots were ordered to keep flying missions in the miserable weather, to continue searching for any threats from the enemy.

For Harold, however, his flying days were over; not by plan, but that's just how things worked out. During the time spent in Guisberg, his observing missions were all ground-based. The three forward observers assigned to each battery undertook the spotting flights, while Harold concentrated on establishing suitable observation positions (OP's) in the mountainous territory around the Deuce's sector.

"I had a good OP overlooking the valley in front of us," Harold relates. "There was this big barn with a peaked roof, and we built a platform up in the hayloft to hold our BC Scope" (the BC or "Battery Commander's" scope was a large, tripod mounted, binocular scope that could measure azimuth and deflection to a target).

Photograph by Third Signal Company. Courtesy of dogfacesoldiers.org

The diminutive size of the Grasshopper observation aircraft is very apparent in the above photograph. A benefit of the lightweight airframe, however, was the capability to operate from snow-covered clearings, close to the front lines.

"We cut a hole high up in the wall of the barn for the two scope arms. It gave us a good view of the goings-on down below and across the valley."

"I put another OP on a hill across another valley to our right, about a mile away, and connected it by telephone wire to the OP in the barn. We could observe the same area from both OP's, so if I saw a target on the road across the valley, like some trucks, I could call the other OP and ask them if they saw the trucks, too. Then we could triangulate the target location and drop in some real accurate fire."

Targets weren't too plentiful during daylight hours, however; the Germans were aware that Harold and others were watching for any sign of movement. Consequently, Harold made sure the battalion could also strike out at night.

"We knew the range to the road, had it zeroed in. We knew the Germans were using the road mostly when it was dark, so we would send a few shells over at night whenever we thought it was being used."

"I don't know if it did any good, but we at least probably had them wondering if and when they would get pelted when they used the road."

Even with the cold and the snow, both sides continued to probe the line, but no major attacks were initiated by the Americans or Germans. Still, occasional enemy targets were sighted, but the rationing of ammunition limited the fire missions that could be undertaken.

Harold Brown Collection

Guisberg, France, where Harold Brown and the 202nd Field Artillery Battalion spent two months in early 1945.

WINTER IN THE VOSGES MOUNTAINS

Photograph by Third Signal Company.   Courtesy of dogfacesoldiers.org

During the winter of 1944/45, contact with the enemy was predominantly limited to small patrols and firing for harassment. In the photograph above, a GI prepares to fire a bazooka rocket towards the German lines.

Photograph by Third Signal Company. Courtesy of dogfacesoldiers.org

This American crew of an armored 105mm howitzer is busy building a log-reinforced position in the Vosges Mountains. With the news that further offensive action was delayed due to supply shortages, many GI's worked hard at making their "winter quarters" as secure and comfortable as possible.

Therefore, much of the additional time was spent clearing heavy snow from the gun and survey positions, dodging frequent counter-battery fire from the Germans, and painting the vehicles and howitzers white while taking care of any deferred maintenance.

Physical conditioning, although unintended, was provided by using long lines of men to bring supplies into the positions as the condition of the snowy ground and frozen roads prevented supply trucks from delivering their goods directly to the Deuce's tents and emplacements.

Even the normally-surefooted M-5 tracked prime movers had trouble on the icy roads. Cleats to improve the "cats" tread grip were ordered, but as was so often the case with urgently needed items in World War II, the cleats didn't arrive until after the spring thaw.

☆   ☆   ☆

Throughout early-1945, nearby field artillery battalions were pulled off of the line one-by-one, and sent to rest centers for a few weeks; not so with the Deuce.

Morale in the 202nd Field Artillery Battalion took a hit as Harold and the men remained on the line at Guisberg through the rest of January, all of February, and into March, still firing daily at the German positions in their sector, still out scouting in the air and on the ground, still dealing with the cold and the snow. There would be no

Photograph by Third Signal Company.   Courtesy of dogfacesoldiers.org

A typical road in the Vosges Mountains during Winter 1944/45.

mental and physical relief for them, no moving off the line for even a brief period.

Consequently, some of the men began showing the strains of being in combat for seven months straight. Harold remembers one 2nd lieutenant in particular who broke under the pressure.

"One day I was out on a forward observing mission with him," Harold says. "We spotted some German troops out in front of us. There were thirty to forty of them, and they were in a 'vee' formation, advancing down a hillside."

"We calculated the coordinates of their location, and I told the lieutenant to call the numbers in for a fire mission. But all of a sudden he got real emotional, he said he couldn't do it, couldn't call in the mission...combat fatigue, I suppose. So I called it in, and we broke up the advance of that group."

"I sent him back to the Battalion, and upon arriving he immediately began digging a foxhole in the frozen ground. HQ sent him to the medical battalion and I never saw him again."

"We heard later that, while on a jeep ride, he shot himself in the foot with his carbine. Some guys just couldn't take it, I guess," Harold states sympathetically.

Most of the men of the Deuce held up fairly well, however, and got on with the tasks at hand. Of course they did wish for some time off of the line; a chance to take a

Photograph by Third Signal Company.   Courtesy of dogfacesoldiers.org

U.S. Sherman tanks sporting their winter camouflage. The Deuce whitewashed its vehicles in a similar manner during the harsh winter of 1944/45.

WINTER IN THE VOSGES MOUNTAINS

warm shower, to wash their filthy uniforms, and if they were lucky, to see a USO show...but it was not to be.

★   ★   ★

After two months at Guisberg, the bitter winter weather of early-1945 slowly began to moderate. Although snow still covered the ground, the days were growing warmer, and the men, like the icy roads, were finally thawing out. Most importantly, however, the supply situation was greatly improved, and the Allied armies could now continue the push east.

The 202nd Field Artillery Battalion was ready to participate in the spring offensive, the long-planned move into Germany.

And they hoped and prayed that it would lead to the end of the war.

Photograph courtesy of Rich Heller   warfoto.com

German-born entertainer Marlene Dietrich gives the GI's of the 3rd Infantry Division something to holler about as she flashes the Division patch at a USO show behind the front lines. The popular Dietrich was a fervent anti-Nazi who was a favorite of American servicemen during WWII. Unfortunately, Harold Brown and most of his fellow artillerymen never had an opportunity to see a USO performance as they remained in combat for over 10 months.

Photograph by Third Signal Company. Courtesy of dogfacesoldiers.org

*GI's of the U.S. 3rd Infantry Division.
Faucogney, France.*

Chapter 15

With the 3ʳᵈ Infantry

★ ★ ★ ★ ★ ★ ★ ★

At 0100 on March 15, 1945, the howitzers of the 202ⁿᵈ Field Artillery Battalion unleashed the first of what was to be a one-day record of 1,819 rounds fired at enemy targets.

The famed U.S. 3ʳᵈ Infantry Division, the "Rock of the Marne," was preparing to jump-off and attack the German lines, to commence at last the spring offensive that all hoped would bring about an end to hostilities on the European continent.

★ ★ ★

Following many months of brutal combat in North Africa and Italy, the 3ʳᵈ Infantry Division stormed the beaches of the Riviera during Operation DRAGOON, the invasion of southern France in August 1944. Attached to

HOWITZERS, GRASSHOPPERS, AND THE HOLY RIGHT HAND

General Patch's U.S. Seventh Army, the seasoned, hard-fighting GI's of the 3rd ID steadily battled their way north along the Rhone River valley, and in September 1944 they reached the Vosges Mountains.

After swinging east towards Germany, the harsh weather and bold German offensives of Winter 1944/45 put a halt to the 3rd ID's advances. Like the Deuce, they passed the early months of 1945 in near-stationary positions, probing the German lines, waiting for the resumption of the push to the east.

After 18 consecutive months of fighting at the front of Allied advances, the infantrymen of the 3rd ID weren't looking forward to further combat. Like many American soldiers, they were weary of the killing, the filth and the fear that they encountered daily. Nevertheless, they realized they still had a job to do, and, like Harold, most of men just wanted to get on with it, defeat the Nazi's, and then go home. The spring offensive was the next step on that path.

Consequently, as the American artillery barrage on the German positions slackened, the 3rd ID GI's doggedly rose up out of their foxholes and shelters, and moved out toward the enemy positions. Resistance was strong from the German defenders, yet the attacking GI's persevered, surged forward, and broke through the enemy line. By the afternoon of the next day, March 16th, the Deuce was obliged

Photograph by Third Signal Company.   Courtesy of dogfacesoldiers.org

GI's poke around an abandoned German Sturmgeschutz IV in the town of Lohr, approximately 20 miles south of Guisberg. American soldiers were constantly on the lookout for souvenirs, but as Harold Brown had seen, booby traps were always a danger, and great care had to be taken when examining anything the enemy had left behind.

to disengage from the battle as the Germans had retreated out of range of the Battalion's guns.

The Deuce's howitzers were repeatedly redeployed over the next three days as the 202nd FA Bn kept pace with the attack. The 3rd Infantry Division's soldiers kept up steady pressure on the retreating enemy, and by March 18th the advance had progressed 21 miles from Guisberg...and out of French territory.

★　　★　　★

Harold was now over the German border, looking down on the defensive components of the Siegfried Line, Hitler's Westwall. This line of fortifications-in-depth ran nearly the entire length of Germany's western border, and its obstacles of extensive minefields, deep anti-tank ditches, and 3' to 4' tall cement "dragon's teeth" were an impediment to the continuation of the American advance. The Siegfried Line had to be crossed, and the Deuce would play a major role in the breaching of it just south of the city of Zweibrücken.

Tasked with clearing the Siegfried obstacles were the combat engineers assigned to the 3rd Infantry Division, and they in turn came to the 202nd Field Artillery Battalion for support with their mission. Harold was in attendance at the Battalion staff meeting between the engineers and the Deuce.

U.S. Army Signal Corps

The Siegfried Line.
This collection of obstacles and hazards stretched nearly the entire length of Germany's western border.

HOWITZERS, GRASSHOPPERS, AND THE HOLY RIGHT HAND

U.S. Army Signal Corps

Dragon's teeth obstacles along the Siegfried Line. These cement obstacles, three to four feet in height, prevented the passage of tanks and vehicles. As such, routes through the Line had to be blasted by the U.S. Army Engineers. The Deuce was called upon to provide suppressing fire while the Engineers carried out their hazardous task.

Photograph by Third Signal Company.   Courtesy of dogfacesoldiers.org

A German pillbox guards a section of the Siegfried Line.

"The engineers figured they could blow the dragon's teeth and fill the ditches if they were given some cover," he relates. "So they asked us to fire on the Germans, to shell them steadily to force their soldiers to stay under cover."

"If we could keep the rifle fire off of the engineers' mine detectors, demolition teams and the heavy equipment operators, they said they could breach the Line in 45 minutes."

The artillerymen of the Deuce were delighted to honor the engineers' request, and soon the first of nearly 1,700 155mm howitzer rounds began falling on the Germans in and behind the Siegfried Line.

Fire, dirt and chunks of flying cement quickly filled the air as shell after shell hit the fortifications. Chemical rounds were also laid in, the smoke from which prevented the enemy from sighting on the engineers as they cautiously moved up through the mine fields that were sewn in front of the anti-tank ditches and concrete obstacles.

The GI's operating the mine detectors worked quickly, and as soon as there were safe corridors through the mine fields, bulldozers were brought forward to fill in the ditches. Next, the engineers placed demolition charges amongst the dragon's teeth and other concrete obstacles. When the explosives were in place and all the men back under cover, the charges were blown. It was quick, efficient work under fire, and Harold says the engineers kept their word.

Photograph by Third Signal Company.   Courtesy of dogfacesoldiers.org

The effects of concentrated U.S. artillery fire and Engineer demolition charges upon the dragon's teeth of the Siegfried Line.

Photograph by Third Signal Company.   Courtesy of dogfacesoldiers.org

Engineers attached to the U.S. 3rd Infantry Division sweep a roadside for mines. The Germans responded to the success of the metal detectors by constructing mines from wood, making them extremely difficult, if not impossible, to detect.

"They told us it would take them 45 minutes to breach the line," he states, "and sure enough, within an hour our troops were headed across."

★ ★ ★

There remained entrenched Germans to deal with on the other side of the Siegfried Line, but the GI's had ways of dealing with them, one of which didn't require the use of ammunition or explosives.

"Sometimes when there was an enemy pillbox or bunker in the way, the engineers were called to bring one of the bladed bulldozers forward," explains Harold. "The driver would raise the blade to protect himself from rifle and machine gun fire, and slowly approach the enemy emplacement."

"The German soldiers were then given a chance to surrender, and if they didn't, the blade operator would approach the gun openings of the bunker and pile dirt up around it so they couldn't shoot out. Then he would proceed to bury the whole thing."

"It worked pretty well, though a lot of those Germans were buried inside their emplacements."

For some reason, where the threat of shells and bullets failed, a pile of dirt succeeded.

★ ★ ★

Photograph courtesy of Rich Heller   warfoto.com

A German pillbox on the Siegfried Line.

Photograph by Third Signal Company.   Courtesy of dogfacesoldiers.org

U.S. Army Engineers put a bulldozer to work clearing an anti-tank barricade from a street in Mutzig, France. When the Siegfried Line was assaulted, Harold Brown looked on as the Engineers used these machines to neutralize German pillboxes.

Photograph courtesy of Rich Heller warfoto.com

Aerial view of a breach made in the Siegfried Line by the engineers of the U.S. 3rd Infantry Division. The anti-tank ditch is visible behind the dragon's teeth obstacles, as is the dirt fill that allowed vehicles to pass over the ditch.

U.S. Army Signal Corps

GI's of the United States Army move up through the Siegfried Line in March of 1945.

HOWITZERS, GRASSHOPPERS, AND THE HOLY RIGHT HAND

Passing quickly through the breaches in the Siegfried Line, the 3rd Infantry Division GI's set-off to the northeast, in the direction of the city of Kaiserlautern. The Americans were on the move once again, and hoped to bring their superior mobility into play, just as they did after the August 1944 breakout from Normandy. Further impetus was provided in the knowledge that the Rhine River lay only 70 miles distant. Being the final natural barrier between the Allied advance and the heart of Germany, the close proximity of the river stirred the GI's onward, and the pace of the advance quickened.

The Germans, by comparison, were thrown off-balance by the American assault, and fell back in disarray, offering little in the way of organized resistance. Hitler's "supermen" gave ground steadily, even though GI boots, tires and tank treads were now moving over the home soils of the *Fatherland*. With hundreds of thousands of men facing the Russians in the east, the German Army simply could not concentrate enough men and equipment to halt the U.S. forces advancing from the west.

Time, it seems, was running out for the Thousand Year Reich.

Photograph courtesy of Rich Heller   warfoto.com

A 3rd Infantry Division mortar crew in the city of Kehl, just over the German border and near the Siegfried Line. The mortarmen have a temporary emplacement set up, and their aiming stakes are visible in front of their weapon. The Deuce also employed aiming stakes, though of a larger variety.

Photograph by Third Signal Company.   Courtesy of dogfacesoldiers.org

The wide, swift Rhine River, last natural obstacle to the heart of Germany.

Chapter 16

Assaulting the Rhine

★ ★ ★ ★ ★ ★ ★ ★

Once they had breached Hitler's vaunted Siegfried Line, the hard-hitting GI's of the 3rd Infantry Division pushed steadily forward for seven days, claiming town after town from the German Wehrmacht. Consequently, the 70 miles to the Rhine were covered much more rapidly than anyone expected.

"The Germans didn't defend their own country as determinedly as they did France," Harold states. "We had a much easier time of it once we crossed the German border. I don't know if it was due to them not wanting their own towns reduced to rubble, or if they just didn't have much fight left in them."

"Frankly, I think a lot of Germans, both soldiers and civilians, just wanted the war to be over."

★ ★ ★

Photograph by Third Signal Company. Courtesy of dogfacesoldiers.org

A street in the city of Zweibrücken, Germany, which lay just beyond the defenses of the Siegfried Line.

ASSAULTING THE RHINE

Only a week after crossing over the Siegfried Line, Harold found himself on the outskirts of the rubble-strewn city of Worms, along the western bank of the Rhine. It was March 25, 1945, and the 202nd Field Artillery Battalion had been chosen to be the first artillery battalion to advance over the wide river.

Gazing over at the German-held eastern bank, Harold wondered how easily the Deuce would be able to cross this massive natural barrier. Up and down the river the retreating Germans had received orders to blow every bridge prior to the arrival of the Americans, and to make a stand on the eastern side, to not allow the Americans to cross and establish a bridgehead.

In the minds of many on both sides of the conflict, the Rhine River was the last great barrier separating the Third Reich from the defeat which most realized was inevitable. To effect the final downfall, however, the river had to be crossed and the eastern bank cleared of German resistance.

★ ★ ★

Assaulting the Rhine and the German defenders entrenched on the eastern side would fall once again to the GI's of the 3rd Infantry Division. Complicating matters, the massive stone Nibelungenbrücke Bridge over the Rhine had been destroyed by the retreating Germans five days earlier, so the assault troops of the 3rd ID would have to cross by boat.

To increase the GI's chances of success and to minimize casualties, the crossing would be undertaken at night. XV Corps HQ decided that the Deuce's howitzers, along with most other available artillery, would support the assault. Accordingly, the guns were called forward and deployed along the American line, and the final few hours of daylight were spent registering the guns on targets on the far bank.

When evening came, the guns fell silent. The American soldiers patiently bided their time...some men trying to catch a little sleep...many too nervous to do so.

Assault teams gathered as twilight turned to darkness, and preparations were finalized for the night crossing of the Rhine.

Engineers carried assault boats up to the western bank, ready to ferry the first wave of assault troops to the far side of the river. Materials necessary to build a pontoon bridge were moved up as well. The bridging of the Rhine would begin as soon as possible, for the only way to quickly move large quantities of troops and equipment across the river would be via a span; boats and ferries would not be sufficient.

ASSAULTING THE RHINE

The Germans detected all of the movement on the U.S side of the river, however, and at 30 minutes to midnight, enemy artillery shells began falling all along the American positions.

Naturally, the GI's gathered along the riverbank wanted to take cover from the incoming shells, but the preparations for the crossing could not be halted if the attack was to proceed. Therefore the assault troops of the 3rd ID and the engineers huddled low behind the river's edge, waiting anxiously for the order to head across.

★ ★ ★

At 0150 on the morning of March 26, 1945, the U.S. artillery massed along the western bank of the Rhine opened fire. The American side of the river flashed with hundreds of tongues of orange flame as round after round headed for German positions.

Ten minutes later the Germans responded with heavy counter-fire, targeting the riverbank and the flashes from the American artillery. Undeterred, return fire from the Deuce and other American artillery units did not slacken, and for 40 minutes the German-held east bank was pummeled with 12,000 rounds of artillery.

At 0230, as scheduled, the 3rd Infantry Division GI's formed up around their assigned assault boats. Each craft held seven infantrymen and two engineers, and the men

Photograph by Third Signal Company.   Courtesy of dogfacesoldiers.org

These are the assault boats used by the Engineers to ferry the 3rd Infantry Division GI's across the Rhine River in the early morning attack on March 26, 1944.

quickly picked the light-weight craft up, and carried them down to the river's edge. Without hesitating, the GI's pushed the boats into the water and swiftly climbed in. Almost immediately the boats began receiving enemy rifle and machine gun fire from the right flank, the riverbank around the east tower of Nibelungenbrücke Bridge. American riflemen and machine gunners promptly returned fire, trying to take some of the heat off of the men in the river.

As enemy tracers zipped overhead and splashed into the water around them, the soldiers of the assault teams huddled low in the boats while the engineers pulled the starter cords on the outboard motors. The motors chugged, caught, then coughed to life, and the boats were slowly nosed into the river's current.

Then, as planned, the U.S. artillery shifted fire, and began "walking" shells to targets back inland from the river; the bombardment of the German-held riverbank was complete. It would be up to the individual foot soldiers to seize the eastern shore from the enemy.

★   ★   ★

Artillery flashed brightly and rifles cracked amidst the shouts of men all throughout the early-morning darkness, while in the murky waters the determined engineers ferried wave after wave of GI's over the river. In the shadowy night it was hard to tell how well the attack was progressing, if at all.

However, as dawn broke over the Rhine on March 26, 1945, and German small-arms fire dissipated, it became apparent that the night crossing had gone well. For the time being at least, the American GI's had established a firm bridgehead on the far side of the river.

The infantrymen were steadily pushing east as well as along the banks of the river to the north and south, expanding the bridgehead and further securing the crossing point. Sporadic German artillery fire continued, but most of it ceased at 0605 when a flight of four P-47 Thunderbolts flew over to provide ground-attack support. The German artillerymen were well aware that if their position wasn't known already, it would most certainly be spotted from the air if they continued firing. They and their guns would then fall prey to the deadly American *Jabos*, as they referred to the USAAF fighter-bombers. Therefore, as the Thunderbolt flight circled the eastern side of the Rhine, the enemy artillery fire abruptly ceased.

☆   ☆   ☆

With the German guns quieted, and the hazards of incoming artillery shells neutralized, the American engineers were finally able to concentrate fully on the task at hand: moving men and equipment across the Rhine.

ASSAULTING THE RHINE

Supplies and reinforcements were needed at the point of the advance, but until a bridge could be assembled, everything had to cross the river by boat. Small vehicles and trailer-loads of supplies required more than a motor boat, so the engineers constructed "rafts" to float these items across the water. The rafts were cobbled together from a section of bridge treadway which was lashed to the tops of five "pontons" (also called "pontoons") outfitted with outboard motors. Jeeps and small trailers could be driven onto the treadways, powered across the river, and then driven off on the opposite bank.

While this method of transport worked well for light loads, the American heavy equipment, artillery, trucks and armor required something far more substantial. They, including the 202nd Field Artillery Battalion, remained stuck on the western bank of the Rhine until the engineers bridged the river.

At 0600, a few minutes before the appearance of the P-47's that would silence the German artillery, the bridge-building effort was commenced by the engineers of the 85th Engineer Heavy Ponton Battalion ("Ponton Battalion" is correct; not "Pontoon Battalion").

As the engineers began the construction of the bridge, DUKW amphibious trucks along with the jury-rigged ponton rafts ran steady circuits back and forth across the river, shuttling troops, supplies and light vehicles to the eastern bank. These small transports were utilized on the return

Photograph by Third Signal Company. Courtesy of dogfacesoldiers.org

One of the "rafts" that was cobbled-together by the 85th Engineers for crossing the Rhine River. Until the ponton bridge was completed, the rafts remained the only means of transporting light vehicles to the far side.

crossing also, for the 3rd Infantry Division GI's were steadily expanding the size of the bridgehead, and there were plenty of wounded Americans, as well as German POW's, to bring back to the western side of the Rhine.

Harold was observing all of this activity with a bit of amazement, especially the building of the bridge.

"That was one of the *greatest* things I saw during the war," he says, "those engineers laying that bridge across the Rhine."

"They had these trucks loaded with all this equipment, and they would drive down the riverbank to the bridge site, peel the stuff off, and put it all together, one section at a time. They used these big pontoons as support, and laid the bridge treadways on top of the pontoons."

"Once one section was done, more pontoons were brought out, and another section of treadway was trucked out and laid into place. It was amazing to watch."

As the engineers continued their bridge building, Harold was ordered to scout out a position on the far bank for the 202nd Field Artillery Battalion.

"As soon as the bridge was completed, we were scheduled to be the first artillery battalion across the river," he relates. "The planners wanted us to get into position to support the continuing attack without the river in the way. We'd rather have it and all of the riverbank congestion behind us."

Photograph courtesy of Milt L. O'Barr Collection

Four GI bridge builders from the 85th Engineer Heavy Ponton Battalion. In the words of Harold Brown, watching these men bridge the Rhine River was "one of the greatest things I saw during the war."

ASSAULTING THE RHINE

Photograph courtesy of Milt L. O'Barr Collection

Pontons loaded on trucks of the 85th Engineers. Harold Brown marveled at the speed with which these craft were employed to build a span across the Rhine River. When completed, the ponton bridge could support the weight of a 37-ton Sherman tank.

HOWITZERS, GRASSHOPPERS, AND THE HOLY RIGHT HAND

Prior to crossing the Rhine, Harold wanted to get a view of the terrain on the far bank so he would be able to find an acceptable location quickly.

"I was looking around for a vantage point that was up high, so I could get a better view than was possible from the riverbank," he explains. "The nearest structure was the tower of the old stone bridge."

The once-picturesque Nibelungenbrücke Bridge was anchored on each bank by imposing turreted towers that straddled the roadway. Though constructed at the turn of the 20th Century, the bridge nonetheless had the look of a medieval castle, built with large stones and a tall, tiled roof. The Germans had demolished the span across the river, but the massive towers still stood at either end. The tower on the western bank looked promising to Harold, and it rose up close-by, just 100 yards to the south of where the ponton bridge was going up.

The tower was surrounded by piles of damaged stonework from the effects of the German demolition charges, but Harold decided to see if he could get into it.

"I was careful as I approached the tower," he relates, "for we were now receiving occasional enemy artillery fire from across the river as our air cover had departed."

"I also didn't know who might be in the tower or the rubble around it. I assumed it had been cleared, but you never know."

As Harold was aware, earlier in the morning and 15 minutes prior to the launching of the assault boats, a sniper

Author's Collection

The Nibelungenbrücke Bridge over the Rhine River, outside of the German city of Worms. The massive stone bridge is pictured as it existed prior to the German retreat across the river. The center spans were blown before the American forces could attempt a crossing. To observe the eastern bank, Harold Brown climbed the tower on the American side of the Rhine (tower on the right of the photograph).

had been spotted in the other bridge tower on the opposite bank, firing on the GI's amassed along the river's edge. A handful of armored artillery was brought up to the riverbank, and they fired into the tower, blasting large holes in the structure. It wasn't known if they got the sniper, but the firing from the tower had ceased for the time being. Harold's sense of caution, therefore, was well-founded.

"I climbed 30 or 40 feet up the steep road embankment," he continues, "and snuck around the side of the tower, staying close to the wall. There was a doorway with some stairs inside, so I headed in."

"I went up a ways until there was a window that faced the river. From there I had a good view across the Rhine. Through my field glasses I viewed what looked like suitable terrain for the battalion, to the north of the bridge."

"Satisfied with what I saw, I was getting ready to head back down when I looked below where I was standing, and on the next level down there was a lieutenant sprawled out on the stone floor...dead. I don't know if he was the victim of a sniper or artillery because I couldn't get to him from where I was."

The fallen GI was just another reminder that death could come anytime or anywhere. Like Harold, the lieutenant may have been scouting out the far bank, but unfortunately he was spotted, possibly by a sniper located in the opposite tower.

Leaving the lieutenant's body for the Graves Registration unit, Harold descended the tower, and with

Photograph courtesy of Milt L. O'Barr Collection

Walter Skulski of the 85th Engineers stands at the base of one the towers on the Nibelungenbrücke Bridge. It is possible that this is the same doorway that Harold Brown passed through on his way up to observe the far side of the Rhine.

HOWITZERS, GRASSHOPPERS, AND THE HOLY RIGHT HAND

even greater caution than before, he hugged the wall outside as he made his way through the stonework.

After carefully looking around he decided the coast was clear, and hustled down the road embankment to make his way back to the river.

★ ★ ★

Working from both sides of the Rhine, the industrious Americans had built the ponton bridge more than halfway across the water by midday. In a few hours the wide river would be spanned, and the Deuce would be traveling across courtesy of the handiwork of the 85th Engineers. That being the case, it was time for Harold to scout out the far bank.

He walked down to the river's edge with Major Glenn Parmer, the battalion S-3 (Operations Officer) who ran the Fire Direction Center. Major Parmer would accompany Harold onto the eastern bank in search of an open, unobstructed site.

"We took a motorboat across the Rhine right around noon," Harold says. "I wasn't too worried about enemy fire because the Germans seemed to be concerned with another bridge to our north. We watched them pelt it throughout the day." (Two other bridges were being constructed that day; one north of Worms, the other south of where Harold was. These other two bridges were built on inflated rubber rafts, light-duty spans that were unable to support heavy vehicles.)

Harold Brown Collection

Major Glenn Parmer lines up for chow in Europe. He and Harold Brown took a boat to the far side of the Rhine in order to scout out a position for the Deuce's howitzers.

Harold and Major Parmer made it across without incident, and soon they were walking cautiously along the eastern bank, looking for the area Harold had previously spotted from the bridge tower.

"We found a suitable location for the three batteries, a couple of hundred yards in from the river," Harold relates. "Major Parmer and I estimated where we would direct the vehicles to the spot, then, our mission complete, we went back across the Rhine and reported back to Colonel Lewis."

"All we had to do now was just wait until the bridge was completed."

Only a little over four hours later, and a mere 10 hours after construction began, the last treadway was laid into position and the Rhine River was bridged. Using 131 flat-bottomed pontons, the hard-working GI's of the 85th Engineer Heavy Ponton Battalion had constructed a stout span 1,047 feet in length, one that could even support a Sherman tank.

☆   ☆   ☆

At 1620, the Deuce-O-Deuce formed up along the riverbank, and set-off across the Rhine.

"It was a funny ride across", Harold remembers. "The pontoons would sink down as you passed over, then rise back up as you passed. The engineers made sure all of the vehicles were spaced at appropriate intervals so as to not swamp the pontoons. Luckily, we didn't have any problems crossing."

"When we got to the other side, I directed the batteries into the positions we had scouted out. Within no time, they were set up and ready to go."

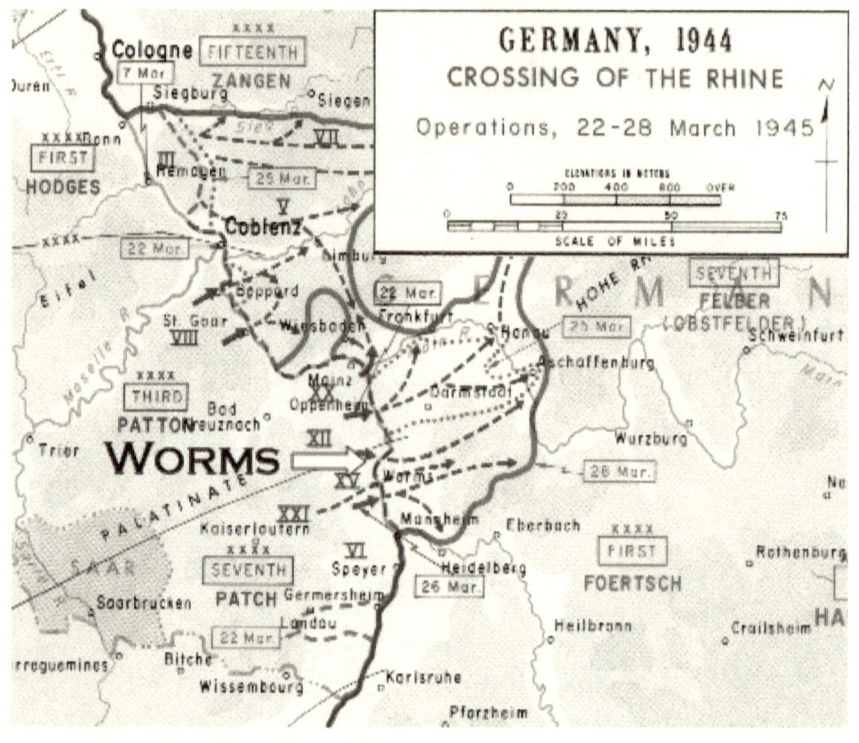

United States Army

On March 26, 1945, Harold Brown and the 202nd Field Artillery Battalion crossed the mighty Rhine River east of the city of Worms, Germany.

Photograph by Third Signal Company. Courtesy of dogfacesoldiers.org

A 155mm howitzer begins its "funny ride" over the Rhine River, courtesy of the 85th Engineers Heavy Ponton Battalion. Harold Brown and the Deuce rode over this bridge soon after it was completed. The east tower of the Nibelungenbrücke Bridge is across the river. Just prior to the American nighttime boat assault, a German sniper began firing from one of the windows in the tower. American artillery was brought forward, and the sniper was silenced. Close inspection of the photograph reveals shell holes on the left side of the tower, just above the stone arch.

Photograph by Third Signal Company.   Courtesy of dogfacesoldiers.org

A U.S. Army M10 Tank Destroyer heads across the Rhine.

ASSAULTING THE RHINE

Image courtesy of dogfacesoldiers.org

The Stars and Stripes trumpets the crossing of the Rhine. Harold Brown and the Deuce crossed the last, great natural barrier to the heart of Germany just below the lower arrow in the map shown above.

Photograph by Third Signal Company.   Courtesy of dogfacesoldiers.org

Heading away from the front, a truckload of German POW's passes a Sherman tankdozer in Lohr, Germany.

Chapter 17

Bread, Butter, and POW's

★ ★ ★ ★ ★ ★ ★ ★

With the mighty Rhine behind them, Harold and the men of the Deuce were now on their way deep into Germany. When asked if it felt different to be on the home soil of the enemy, Harold says no, it was just a continuation of the experiences of the past nine months. He and the other GI's were still on the move, still ducking enemy fire, still hoping for the day when the war would end and they could all go home.

Changing for the better, though, were sleeping arrangements for the 202nd Field Artillery Battalion. Surprisingly, now that they had advanced into Germany, sacking-out on the ground or in foxholes became an infrequent occurrence. Often Harold and his fellow GI's would find themselves bunked down with a roof over their heads, inside a clean house, and out of the elements.

"As we traveled through Germany we would hole up in some houses where the Germans were living," Harold relates, "so we could spend a warm night indoors."

How did the local population react to American GI's taking over their beds?

"At first we didn't have much contact at all with German civilians," Harold relates. "Frequently they knew we were coming, so they were usually pretty well hidden when we got to their towns."

Some Germans weren't too thrilled with giving up their beds to the Americans, however, and would initially refuse to leave their houses. Nonetheless, such refusals had little effect on the GI's.

"On occasion, we ran some of them out so we could sleep in their house for a night," Harold explains. "After what we had seen and experienced, it didn't bother us at all to inconvenience the Germans for a night or two."

As the American forces pushed deeper into Germany, many GI's indeed became resentful of the well-kept homes and apparent plentiful food that they encountered along the way. Granted, the major cities of Germany were decimated moonscapes, many buildings nothing but burned-out shells as a result of two years of repeated Allied bombings. But the small towns and countryside of Germany were idyllic settings of peace and normalcy.

BREAD, BUTTER, AND POW'S

This was in stark contrast to the destruction of French towns, and the deprivations suffered by the local populace, that the men had experienced during the drive across France. If a night could be spent inside, out of the chilly spring night air, it was of small concern to the GI's if the German homeowners were put out, for their lives appeared to be untouched by the horrors of the war that had been raging across Europe for over five years.

Sleeping more like a human and less like an animal wasn't the only adjustment tackled by the GI's in spring of 1945. As the fighting progressed even deeper into the heart of Germany, similar changes in the nature of the war were encountered in various other ways.

"It really wasn't an all-out war like we had before," Harold explains. "I remember one time when we had taken over a farmhouse, and we would allow the German farmer to come in to the barn and milk the cows, to take care of his daily chores. We treated his property with respect."

"But in the kitchen," he continues, "there was this big loaf of freshly baked, dark bread...rye bread I guess it was, *and fresh butter...*"

Harold gets a sheepish look on his face, and you can just see the satisfaction coming back in his eyes even though 62 years have passed since he encountered that loaf of German bread!

"We ate the bread *and* the butter," he says with a huge smile, "...and it tasted good, you bet!"

Photograph by Third Signal Company.   Courtesy of dogfacesoldiers.org

Desolate, destroyed and deserted French town...

Photograph by Third Signal Company.   Courtesy of dogfacesoldiers.org

...in stark contrast to a German town that appears to be relatively untouched by the effects of war.

The heartening effect on a soldier's disposition from something as simple as fresh bread and butter, as well as a few hours of sleep indoors, can not be easily discounted. These are "necessities" most people take for granted, but they are things that a soldier on the front lines can usually only dream about.

After sleeping on or in the ground night after night, after fighting, eating and sleeping in the same clothes for weeks on end, after going over a month without the opportunity to bathe, soldiers become removed from what is considered a normal, civilized existence. They will jump at any opportunity to have but a small piece of what has become a luxury to them: a bed, a bath, and some food for their bellies other than dried K-rations, canned C-rations, or the perennial GI "favorite", SPAM...though Harold takes exception to the slam on SPAM.

"I had quite a bit of it, but it wasn't too bad," he says. "Fried SPAM was pretty good!"

Harold also has a little insight to offer on the country-dwelling Germans.

"I guess they could have poisoned us with their food if they wanted to," he says, "but they weren't interested. They just wanted to get the war over with."

"Most of our men didn't treat the German civilians with animosity, but were actually pretty friendly with them; we were all friendly with them. As we moved further into

Photograph by Third Signal Company.   Courtesy of dogfacesoldiers.org

It's chow time for GI's on the front line. It appears that cold, canned C-Rations are the featured menu item of the day.

HOWITZERS, GRASSHOPPERS, AND THE HOLY RIGHT HAND

Photograph by Third Signal Company.   Courtesy of dogfacesoldiers.org

The ruins of the town of Hornbach, targeted on the initial drive into Germany. If retreating Wehrmacht troops attempted to make a stand in a town, American artillery was immediately called in to persuade the enemy to surrender or fall back. As the drive into Germany progressed, Harold Brown observed that more and more of the rural towns were yielded to the Americans without a fight.

Germany, we realized these people were peace-loving. They were just farmers, and they didn't like the war either."

"These country people didn't like Hitler, and a lot of them were really glad we got in there."

★   ★   ★

After a night in the German farmhouse, and following a rare breakfast of fresh eggs, Harold and the Deuce were off again, resuming the push to the east.

With the German defenders falling steadily back towards the heart of Germany, the rapidly pursuing 3rd Infantry Division GI's found themselves moving forward many miles each day, usually stopping at one location for no more than a single night. The howitzers of the 202nd FA Bn kept pace, and were advancing most days just a mile or two behind the infantrymen.

By late March 1945, as the Americans, British and French were pushing through Germany from the west, the Russians were relentlessly driving in from the east, getting ever nearer the Allies ultimate goal, the German capital of Berlin.

All along their advance, the Russian troops were exacting vicious retribution on the German population, reprisals for the horrendous treatment that Russian soldiers and civilians had experienced at the hands of the Nazi's. Word of the Russian onslaught and all it entailed spread quickly throughout Germany, both to the Germans and the Americans.

Harold recognized this fear among the German civilians he encountered, and he realized that most of them were glad to have the Americans as conquerors.

"In many towns we could tell that they were especially relieved that we got to them before the Russians," he recalls. "They'd have the white flags hanging from their windows, sometimes waving to us as we went by."

★   ★   ★

On March 31, 1945, the 202nd Field Artillery Battalion had progressed 35 miles east of the Rhine to the town of Wörth am Main, just to the southeast of Frankfurt. Harold and the men were now 140 miles inside Germany, and less than 375 miles from Berlin. They waited briefly for their turn to cross over the Main River, and struck out to the northeast in the direction of Schweinfurt, the site of the two infamous 1943 daylight bombing raids on the city's ball bearing works that claimed the lives of over 1000 American airmen.

During this advance into Germany, the Deuce would occasionally capture enemy soldiers who were unable to retreat, or who simply wanted to surrender. Under the watchful eyes of GI guards, these Germans were first searched for any hidden weapons, then they were lined up to be questioned about their name, rank, which division

Photograph by Third Signal Company.   Courtesy of dogfacesoldiers.org

A German civilian searches the rubble of a destroyed building in Steinach, Germany. As the Deuce moved further into the heart of Germany, they began to encounter the results of the Allied strategic bombing campaign against German industry. Such destruction stood in sharp contrast to the rural towns the GI's first encountered in Germany, towns which appeared untouched by the war.

HOWITZERS, GRASSHOPPERS, AND THE HOLY RIGHT HAND

they were assigned to, etc. Harold remembers a method of interrogation that was usually very successful.

"All of the prisoners were interviewed to get information," he begins. "Many of them didn't know anything, but a lot of them also were pretty arrogant, and refused to answer."

"The interrogation desk was set up by the mess tent, and if a prisoner refused to answer, he was sent back to the rear of the interrogation line, to be questioned again. Meanwhile, those POW's that did talk were sent to the mess tent to get some food...they were all pretty hungry!"

"The arrogant ones eventually figured out that they wouldn't be eating until they talked, so they caught on pretty quick."

Sometimes German soldiers would try to sneak through the American lines, not to fight, but to make their way home. Though it was possible they could cause trouble later on behind the lines, most of them had decided the war was lost.

"One day we were set up in a treed area, somewhat densely forested, and here comes a man and women walking through the trees," Harold explains. "I noticed his clothes were kind of bulky; he didn't look normal. So I hollered 'Go check that guy out' to a corporal over by where they were coming through."

"He un-shouldered his rifle and stopped the two of them, and sure enough, the man had his German Army uniform on under the civilian clothes."

"I don't know where he and this girl were headed, but we stopped him. I think he was just tired of the war and wanted to get out."

Harold's enemy-in-disguise was just one of a steadily growing group of German POW's whose war had come to an end. Over the next month, Allied troops throughout Germany would encounter similar German soldiers in ever increasing numbers, more than they could even possibly imagine.

☆   ☆   ☆

Following the rapidly advancing GI's of the 3rd Infantry Division, the Deuce rolled quickly through the German countryside, passing through the towns of Lohr am Main, Hammelburg, and Bad-Kissingen.

From this last town, in the first week of April 1945, orders suddenly came through directing the infantry and artillery to immediately swing to the southeast, over the Main River again, this time crossing in the vicinity of Knetzgau. With such a drastic change of direction, the men wondered why they were being shifted 90 degrees, no longer aiming towards Berlin and the advancing Russians, but now towards Bavaria in southern Germany, with Austria beyond.

The answer was that they had been selected for a special mission: their destination was Nuremberg.

Photograph by Third Signal Company.   Courtesy of dogfacesoldiers.org

For them, the war is over.

Photograph by Third Signal Company.   Courtesy of dogfacesoldiers.org

For him, the war is over.

HOWITZERS, GRASSHOPPERS, AND THE HOLY RIGHT HAND

Designated by Hitler as the *Stadt aus die Reichsparteitage*, or City of the Nazi Party Rallies, Nuremberg contained the Nazi Party Rally Grounds, where prior to the outbreak of war, Hitler addressed upwards of one million sympathizers in the sprawling outdoor *Zepplinfeld* arena.

The city was symbolic of Nazi power; here Nazi architect Albert Speer had designed massive buildings built for the sole purpose of expressing Nazi superiority to the world. National Socialist Party ideology permeated the fabric of Nuremberg; the city square was named Adolf Hitler Platz, and Hitler agreed with the mayor of the city who declared it as "the most German of all German cities."

Consequently, Nuremberg was teeming with fanatical Nazis and their supporters, individuals who were willing to die for their Führer...and the Allied command staff wanted the city taken...at all costs.

U.S. Army Signal Corps

A long column of German POW's stretches beyond the view of the camera as they march through a German city in 1945.

Photograph by Third Signal Company.   Courtesy of dogfacesoldiers.org

A local youth gazes upon a disabled German Jagdpanzer 38 tank destroyer in Frankenheim, Germany. As Hitler's forces retreated across Europe, they left a trail of abandoned and destroyed equipment in their wake.

Harold Brown Collection

"Superman" was the word Harold Brown wrote on the back of this photograph, which he picked up in a house he spent the night in while moving through Germany. Harold says the arrogant look of the German officer, one of Hitler's so-called Aryan "Supermen", rubbed him the wrong way, hence the comment he wrote on the photograph.

HOWITZERS, GRASSHOPPERS, AND THE HOLY RIGHT HAND

National Archives

1935 Nazi Party Rally in Nuremberg, Germany. Upwards of one million sympathizers attended Adolf Hitler's speeches at the Rally Grounds.

Chapter 18

Fall of Nuremberg...Death at Dachau

☆ ☆ ☆ ☆ ☆ ☆ ☆ ☆

"Not many towns stand out to me from our march through Germany," Harold states. "But Nuremburg does."

Since their second crossing of the Main River at Knetzgau a week prior, the Deuce had traveled south some 60 miles. On occasion enemy resistance stiffened, but the GI's refused to be stopped. Several German towns realized this, and they capitulated peacefully, without so much as a single shot being fired.

Other towns weren't cognizant of the reality facing Nazism, and were subsequently reduced to rubble by American artillery and bombs in attempt to root out the German defenders.

☆ ☆ ☆

HOWITZERS, GRASSHOPPERS, AND THE HOLY RIGHT HAND

Momentum had been on the Allies side since the Rhine River crossing, and the American men, trucks and armor continued to spread out over an ever-widening area of central Germany in April of 1945. Morale was high, and the GI's knew it really was just a matter of time before the Nazi's were defeated.

Spirits among the U.S. forces did suffer a blow, however, when the news came down that President Franklin Delano Roosevelt had died.

FDR had been a constant fixture in the lives of Americans from the time when he was first elected President in November 1932 during the depths of the Depression. When he died on April 12, 1945, after 13 years in office, for many Americans (even those who did not agree with his policies), it was a strange thought to imagine America without FDR as president.

Gone was the man whose radical social programs had rescued the Nation from the grips of the Great Depression of the 1930's. Gone was Britain's ally, who, with his famous "fireside chats" of 1940 and 1941, vigorously urged isolationist-America to establish itself as the "Arsenal of Democracy" for the purpose of supplying Britain with the tools of war. In late-1940, Britain alone stood against the Nazi tide of conquest, and FDR knew America must help.

Gone was the encouraging, confident leader who, when faced with military defeat after defeat in the dark days of late-1941 and early-1942, pulled America's 130,000,000 people together, and prepared them for the difficult tasks, and many sacrifices, which he knew lay ahead.

Gone was the president whose polio-stricken legs confined him to a wheelchair, but whose mind was resolute and strong. His determination and belief in the righteousness of the Allied cause was infectious, and under his leadership the peoples of the United States were united as they had *never* been before...or since.

Most young GI's had not known a president other than Franklin Roosevelt. The sudden news of his death from a stroke was unexpected, but for the soldiers on the front line, the focus had to remain on the task at hand.

"We were surprised, a bit taken aback," Harold remembers of that day, "but we had to continue on with what we had to do."

While the homefront mourned FDR's passing, the 202nd Field Artillery Battalion continued fighting the war, the miles to Nuremburg lessening with each passing day.

By April 17, 1945, Captain Harold Brown and the Deuce were on the outskirts of the Nazi-held city.

★ ★ ★

Clouds of smoke and dust hung in a pall over the city. Gunfire cracked continuously, and both outgoing and incoming artillery shells moaned overhead. The Germans had established a defensive ring around Nuremberg, and they were putting up a determined resistance.

Batteries of the feared 88mm FlaK gun were dug in north of the city, firing into the advancing 3rd Infantry Division GI's. The 12 howitzers of the 202nd Field Artillery Battalion were called in for a fire mission, ordered to take out 12 of the German 88's that had been spotted in a field.

As they had done so many times over the past 10 months, the men of the Deuce quickly moved the batteries into position, unhooked the guns from the prime movers, set up the aiming circles and stakes, adjusted the howitzers to the initial target coordinates, and upon command fired the initial registration rounds.

A forward observer with another artillery unit had a direct view of the enemy batteries, and he adjusted the Deuce's fire until it was right on target. When the order "Fire for effect" was given, the 155mm howitzers sent their high-explosive shells directly onto the German batteries. Shellfire from the 88's ceased immediately, and the guns of the Deuce were shifted to another target.

Later the next day after the Germans had withdrawn, the men of the 202nd Field Artillery Battalion had the chance to see the direct results of their artillery fire, an opportunity which did not present itself very often during the war. They piled into trucks and drove down to the field where the 12 German 88's were deployed.

FALL OF NUREMBERG...DEATH AT DACHAU

The sight which awaited them would bring a smile to any artilleryman's face. The accuracy of the 155's was spot-on, and Harold and the cannoneers examined two 88's that had received direct hits, seven others that had been put out of action by shrapnel, and the final three guns that the Germans had rendered inoperable before they pulled back towards Nuremberg. The field held undeniable evidence that the years of training had been worth the effort.

With the knowledge that they had saved the lives and limbs of numerous GI's, the men of the 202nd FA Bn, feeling perhaps a little cockier now than before, returned to their batteries and awaited further orders.

★ ★ ★

Combat had evolved into treacherous street-by-street fighting as the 3rd ID infantrymen pushed the enemy from the outskirts of Nuremberg. The German main line of resistance was now the city itself, and in the hopes of preventing further destruction and civilian casualties, the Americans issued an ultimatum for the surrender of the city and the troops inside.

Unconcerned with the lives of innocents, the fanatical Nazi defenders refused. As a result, the Deuce joined with other massed U.S. artillery units in unleashing a ferocious artillery barrage onto the doomed city.

Photograph by Third Signal Company. Courtesy of dogfacesoldiers.org

U.S. armor moves cautiously into Nuremberg. German defenders of the city, soldiers and civilians alike, were armed with the highly-effective Panzerfaust, *a bazooka-like anti-tank weapon that proved deadly for American tanks.*

Each unit was assigned a section of Nuremberg to target, and Harold recalls a memorable one that was assigned to the 202nd FA Bn.

"We shelled the big stadium in Nuremberg, where the Nazi's held their rallies," he says. "I could see it from where we were deployed."

As the symbolic center of Nazi power, the entire city was a target, a fact which held especially true for the buildings and landmarks built specifically for the Nazi Party. Recognizing the political significance of Nazi architect Albert Speer's creations, the American commanders believed the structures would be rallying points for the defenders, and fiercely contested. Therefore, the artillery was put to work on the *Zepplinfeld*.

"We shelled it, but I really don't know if there were German troops there or not," Harold says. "Maybe we shelled it just for the heck of it...just to tear up their stadium."

American guns rained destruction down all around the city for three days while the 3rd Infantry Division GI's engaged in vicious house-to-house fighting against Nuremberg's defenders. The city was sacred to the party faithful, and they paid for it with their lives, block-by-block. Like the Third Reich, however, Nuremberg's fate was sealed.

On April 20, 1945, with the majority of its buildings in shambles, the city fell to the Americans.

Photograph by Third Signal Company.   Courtesy of dogfacesoldiers.org

GI's line the grandstand at the Zepplinfeld in Nuremberg. Soon they will unfurl an American flag over the giant swastika above the grandstand. Later, the symbol of the Nazi Party will be blown apart by explosives, forever erasing it from the structure.

Photograph by Third Signal Company.   Courtesy of dogfacesoldiers.org

The Stars and Stripes is raised over Hitler's grandiose forum.

HOWITZERS, GRASSHOPPERS, AND THE HOLY RIGHT HAND

Photograph by Third Signal Company. Courtesy of dogfacesoldiers.org

Hitler's swastika is "kaput".

FALL OF NUREMBERG...DEATH AT DACHAU

U.S. Army Signal Corps

Aerial view of the Zepplinfeld, the site of Hitler's massive rallies in Nuremberg. The structure and grounds exhibit damage, some of which was caused by 155mm howitzer shells of the 202nd Field Artillery Battalion.

HOWITZERS, GRASSHOPPERS, AND THE HOLY RIGHT HAND

Photograph courtesy of Rich Heller warfoto.com

The ruins of Nuremburg, Germany.

Hitler's "Most German of all German cities" fell to the U.S. Army's 3rd Infantry Division after a vicious four-day battle. The howitzers of the Deuce supported the GI's in the street-by-street fight for the city.

FALL OF NUREMBERG...DEATH AT DACHAU

U.S. Army Signal Corps

The extent of the destruction wrought upon Nuremberg is evidenced in this photograph, taken after the battle for the city had ended.

Photograph by Third Signal Company. Courtesy of dogfacesoldiers.org

Another view of Nuremberg's destruction.

FALL OF NUREMBERG...DEATH AT DACHAU

Photograph by Third Signal Company.   Courtesy of dogfacesoldiers.org

Having failed to keep their city out of U.S. hands, German POW's are marched out of Nuremberg.

HOWITZERS, GRASSHOPPERS, AND THE HOLY RIGHT HAND

The date held a twist of irony as April 20 was also Hitler's birthday. As a present from the GI's of the 3rd Infantry Division, as well as Harold and the Deuce, his "most German of all German cities" was wrested from his control forever.

★   ★   ★

April 20, 1945, was also the day the 202nd Field Artillery Battalion was detached from the 3rd Infantry Division. Although they would follow in each others' footsteps through the ending of hostilities, their official "working" relationship was over.

The 202nd FA Bn and the 3rd ID had seen a lot of action together, first in the great spring offensive out of the Vosges Mountains, and then on across the German border. Next they punched through the Siegfried Line, and bridged the mighty Rhine River. Finally, after pushing the Germans through central Germany, they captured the important Nazi city of Nuremberg. All of this was theirs to lay claim to…and they accomplished it in just 37 days.

★   ★   ★

The howitzers of the Deuce were still under the direction of the XV Corps, and if infantry or armored divisions in the XV Corps required artillery support, the Battalion could be assigned to assist them. Consequently, six days after departing the ruins of Nuremberg, Harold and the 202nd Field Artillery Battalion were deployed on a hillside overlooking the Danube River outside the small village of Schweizer Hof.

The GI's of the 42nd "Rainbow" Infantry Division were preparing to cross the river, and the Deuce's big guns were targeting enemy vehicles, troop concentrations, road junctions and buildings on the opposite side. In support of the crossing, the howitzer's 155mm HE shells were soon joined by aircraft of the USAAF which added their bullets and bombs to the rain of deadly metal falling all along the opposite side of the Danube.

From their vantage point on the hillside, Harold and the men of the 202nd FA Bn had a front row seat of the crossing action, as well as a prime view of the effectiveness of American artillery and air power. Hundreds of shells and bombs landed amongst the German lines on and behind the southern riverbank, and the enemy defenses soon lost their cohesiveness. Under the cover provided by this American firepower, the GI's of the 42nd Infantry Division moved across the Danube in DUKW's and assault boats, spread out along the river bank and pushed forward.

As with the Rhine River crossing, the Danube was quickly and efficiently bridged by GI's of the 85th Engineers Heavy Ponton Battalion, and after another "funny ride" over the dipping ponton boats, Harold and the Deuce were once

Photograph courtesy of Milt L. O'Barr Collection

The ponton bridge over the Danube River, constructed by the 85th Engineers. Shortly after firing their howitzers in support of the attack to secure the opposite side, Harold Brown and the Deuce crossed the river on this bridge.

FALL OF NUREMBERG...DEATH AT DACHAU

Photograph by Third Signal Company.   Courtesy of dogfacesoldiers.org

In the center of the photograph is a DUKW, or "duck". These ungainly looking vehicles proved themselves to be one of the greatest American inventions of the war. The amphibious truck was based on the workhorse "Deuce-and-a-half" (2 ½ ton) truck, only this version could transition from truck to boat with minimal effort. Harold Brown watched the DUKW's in action during major river crossings in France and Germany.

again heading south, this time towards the Bavarian capital of Munich.

This southern-Germany city was the site of the 1923 Beer Hall Putsch (*putsch* means "coup" in German) when Hitler and his Nazi Party stormtroopers first tried to take over the country.

As the birthplace of Nazism, support for the Führer was strong in Munich, and it was rumored that Hitler had ordered a National Redoubt, or *Alpenfestung* (Alpine Fortress), to be established in the Bavarian Alps to the south so that the forces of Nazi Germany could fight on from a position of strength. The Allied command was fearful of such a development, and this was one reason why Patch's Seventh Army was directed 90 degrees south earlier in the month.

With less than 70 miles to go from the Danube to the outskirts of Munich, the 202nd Field Artillery Battalion was therefore hot on the heels of the infantrymen of the 42nd Infantry Division as they steadily beat the weakening Germans back towards the city.

★ ★ ★

It was during the advance to Munich when, on May 29, 1945, Harold experienced an event that, for him, brought clarity to why he was far from home fighting Nazism, why he was risking his life to bring freedom to the oppressed peoples of Europe.

U.S. Army Signal Corps

For the first time ever, there is cheering at Dachau concentration camp as American GI's enter the grounds.

"We were on the road, and as I was at the head of the column, I had the freedom to snoop around a little bit as we saw things," he relates.

"I was passing near the town of Dachau, just north of Munich, and I could see a bunch of activity around a fenced-in camp, so I went over to check it out. I saw that the 45th Infantry Division had guards out, and they were freeing the prisoners from this camp."

2 ½ weeks earlier on April 11th, and 250 miles due north of Dachau, the U.S. 6th Armored Division had broken down the gates of the Buchenwald death camp. Word of the horrors they uncovered had spread quickly throughout the American forces in Europe. Many GI's, including Harold, had heard reports detailing what the 6th Armored had found, but most could not even begin to comprehend the extent of the atrocities.

"Well, it looked to me like everything was under control," Harold continues. "There wasn't anything I could do. But I was curious to see what it was like, so I just went and looked."

Harold parked his jeep and took a walk around the camp. "Not wanting to interfere, I didn't snoop in it at all," he says, but one area of the camp drew him over for a closer look. "There were railroad flatcars...loaded with bodies, stacked maybe three or four deep...and they had *lots* of the cars."

FALL OF NUREMBERG...DEATH AT DACHAU

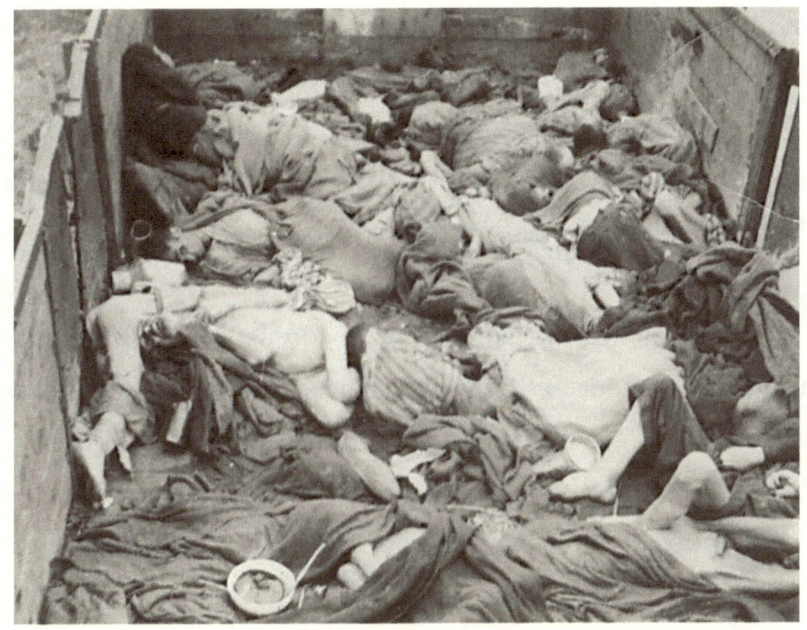

Photograph by Third Signal Company.   Courtesy of dogfacesoldiers.org

<u>*Evidence of the Nazi's "Final Solution"*</u>

A railroad car at Dachau, possibly one that Harold Brown viewed. Many Americans, including the most battle-hardened GI's, were sickened by what they saw and experienced at the Nazi death camps.

"I couldn't figure out why they would have so many. And then it occurred to me that maybe it was because the cremation ovens weren't sufficient enough to keep up with the supply of bodies, so they were backlogged with them."

"Now that's just a theory on my part...I don't know if that's correct. We had heard that they were coming across these camps in several places."

All of the prisoners were dressed in the striped uniforms issued to them by their captors, and as at the other camps, the internees were in a state of starvation.

"They had to be fed for a while to get their weight back," Harold says. "Their ribs showed...they didn't have any meat on their bones at all, and their legs were all shrunken."

Once the results of the Nazi's "Final Solution" were seen firsthand, many veterans who experienced the camps will state that they no longer had any doubts as to why they were in Europe, why they were fighting. Harold is no different.

"That's exactly right," he says. "That's just exactly what came into my mind when I saw it...'Now I know why we came here.'"

FALL OF NUREMBERG...DEATH AT DACHAU

U.S. Army Signal Corps

Freedom at Dachau.

U.S. Army Signal Corps

Concentration camp survivors at Dachau celebrate their liberation. Harold Brown remembers the striped clothing worn by the internees, as well as their emaciated appearance.

FALL OF NUREMBERG...DEATH AT DACHAU

United States Army

Harold Brown's route through Germany and Austria over the last six weeks of World War II is visible on this map. From Worms, Germany at the center of the left side, then east to Nuremberg, south to Dachau and Munich, Germany, and finally southeast to Salzburg and Berchtesgaden, Austria, at the lower right.

HOWITZERS, GRASSHOPPERS, AND THE HOLY RIGHT HAND

National Archives

Adolf Hitler treats Italian dictator Benito Mussolini to a scenic drive through downtown Munich, Germany. By war's end, both men would be dead, along with their grandiose dreams of fascist empires.

Chapter 19

Autobahn to Salzburg

★ ★ ★ ★ ★ ★ ★ ★

After leaving the concentration camp, Harold rejoined the 202nd Field Artillery Battalion's convoy as they rolled south towards Munich.

The following day, April 30, 1945, dawned clear and sunny, a stark contrast to the nightmarish visions he had viewed at Dachau. Mindful of these horrors, Harold focused intently on the day's present task: locating a suitable firing position for the howitzers outside of Munich.

★ ★ ★

Expecting a brutal fight for the city, the Deuce had deployed it's howitzers in position to support the move into Munich. But for once, fire orders were not issued. The city was left nearly undefended, with only small pockets of resistance encountered by the U.S. infantrymen as they moved into Munich. Still, the 42nd Infantry Divisions GI's advanced cautiously, not knowing what might be lurking around the next corner or in the next building.

Like most major German cities, Munich had been heavily bombed by the Allied strategic air offensive. The resulting rubble piles and shells of damaged buildings provided many hiding places for Nazi defenders, but by mid-afternoon it became clear that Munich was not going to be the same as Nuremberg. White flags were flying throughout the city, and many civilians were welcoming the Americans as liberators.

As the Deuce was deployed outside of the city center, some men from the 202nd Field Artillery Battalion decided to explore the outskirts of the downtown area, and just by chance they came across a useful find.

"We had a bunch of photography buffs in our battalion," Harold relates, "and these guys knew a lot about cameras. While snooping around Munich they came across a camera factory."

At the time, the AGFA Kamera-werk was unoccupied as the German employees had fled to places of safety when the Americans approached the city.

"The guys got inside of it," Harold continues, "and found that the factory was full of camera parts and pieces."

Amused by the memory, Harold smiles and tells what his resourceful colleagues did: "Of course they went down the assembly line and made cameras for themselves!"

Photograph courtesy of Rich Heller   warfoto.com

Downtown Munich, Germany, exhibiting the heavy damage that was inflicted by Allied bombing raids. The city was spared further destruction when it was surrendered to American forces. Had the city's defenders resisted, the howitzers of the Deuce would have contributed to the devastation.

Photograph by Third Signal Company.   Courtesy of dogfacesoldiers.org

Wehrmacht General Fehn, accompanied by his truce delegation, surrenders the city of Munich to the U.S. 3rd Infantry Division.

Photograph by Third Signal Company.   Courtesy of dogfacesoldiers.org

The historic Karlstor Gate in Munich's old city center.

Harold Brown Collection

The Deuce's dishwasher, "Doc" Hardin, diligently performs his duty at the Battalion Mess outside of Munich, Germany, in early-May 1945.

Harold has a healthy respect for the German industrial capabilities that existed during World War II, whether the product was a camera or an 88 FlaK gun.

"The Germans had good equipment," he states. "They made good lenses and many other things...they were just a progressive people when it came to manufacturing, I think."

On this day the cameras did the shooting, and the 202nd Field Artillery Battalion's howitzers stood silent.

★　　★　　★

Harold and the Deuce were in for a quiet day, and without a doubt the change was welcome. The war was winding down...the men could feel it.

After 10 months on the front of the Allied advance through Europe, they could finally start imagining the day when they would no longer have to endure freezing nights sleeping on the ground, and eating cold boxed food for meal after meal. No more keeping their ears tuned for the dreaded sound of an incoming German 88, or cautiously eyeing every tree, dark window and pile of rubble for enemy snipers. Things were finally looking up.

The situation had definitely changed for the better on this 30th day of April, 1945. For even though Harold and his fellow GI's wouldn't find out until the next day, in the Führer Bunker deep under the shattered Reichschancellory building in Berlin, Adolf Hitler lay dead. And along with him went his dreams for the Thousand Year Reich.

★ ★ ★

News of Hitler's death had little immediate effect on Harold and the men of the Deuce. "We just kept doing what we needed to do," he recalls. "We didn't do any celebrating. But I suppose the German civilians celebrated; at that point in the war they didn't seem to like him too well."

May 2, 1945, found the 202nd Field Artillery Battalion loaded up and ready to drive through Munich. It was going to be a quick trip, however, without any sightseeing stops.

"We didn't spread out as we went in there," Harold recalls. "We just went on through. They wanted us down in Salzburg."

As was the case with Paris in autumn of 1944, the race was on to see whether troops from the democracies of America, Great Britain and France, or communist Russia would reach certain cities first. The major prize of Berlin had already been ceded to the Russians, but the fate of other major cities and countries had yet to be decided.

The seeds of the Cold War had been sown prior to 1945, and now the governments of the four major Allied partners jockeyed for position in the post-war world which they knew would be upon them any day.

AUTOBAHN TO SALZBURG

Image courtesy of dogfacesoldiers.org

Enough said.

Photograph by Third Signal Company.   Courtesy of dogfacesoldiers.org

With a couple of U.S. Military Policemen (MP's) in a jeep watching the intersection, a streetcar rolls down the street in Munich. When it was time for the Deuce to travel through the city, the debris-free streets made their journey a quick one.

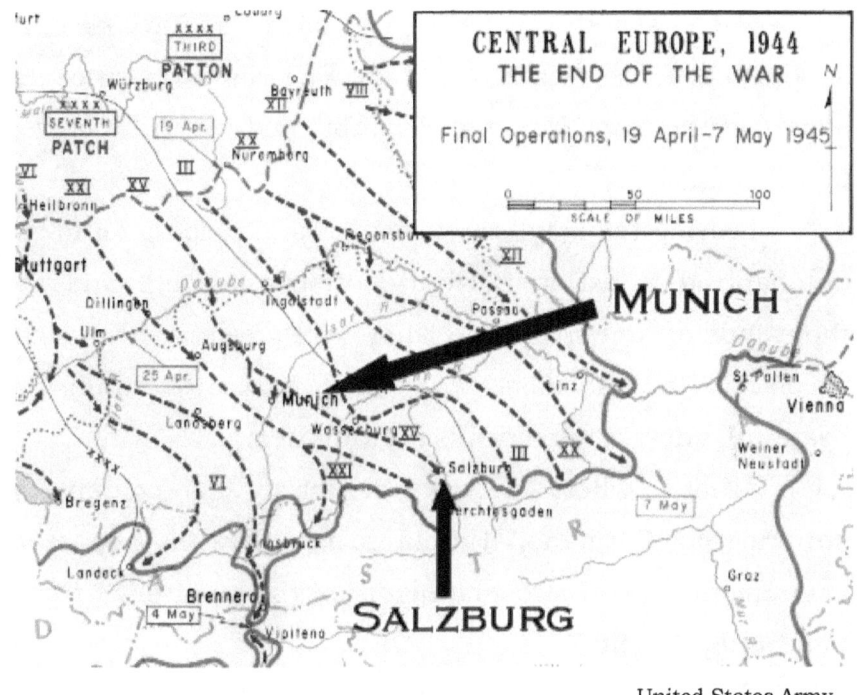

United States Army

The last major movement made by Harold Brown and the 202nd Field Artillery Battalion was from Munich, Germany, to Salzburg, Austria.

HOWITZERS, GRASSHOPPERS, AND THE HOLY RIGHT HAND

★   ★   ★

There was still, however, a sense of military urgency for the U.S. forces heading into the Bavarian Alps since the stories of the Nazi "National Redoubt" had yet to be proven false.

Leaving the small roads behind and turning on to the autobahn that led to Salzburg, Austria, Harold and the thousands of Americans with him were greeted with a sight which lay to rest most fears of a Nazi fortress in the beautiful, snow-capped peaks around them.

"That's where I saw the first big column of surrendering Germans," Harold says, still with a sense of amazement. "They were coming out of the mountains there, *thousands* of them."

"Whoever was in charge sent them up one side of the autobahn towards Munich, and we were on the other side going down towards Salzburg. They filled the entire autobahn. It was quite a sight."

Even though the two enemies were separated from each other by only a narrow median, it was obvious that both sides were tired of fighting, did not wish for confrontation, and in the case of the German soldiers, just wanted to get home.

"They were all peaceful, there didn't seem to be any Germans causing problems," Harold remembers. "We had taken the small arms away from the enlisted men, but we let the German officers and non-coms keep their pistols."

Photograph courtesy of Milt L. O'Barr Collection

The Autobahn between Munich, Germany, and Salzburg, Austria. When traveled by Harold Brown and the Deuce, one side of the roadway was jammed with American vehicles headed south, while the other side, or the median, was crowded with German soldiers on their way back to Germany.

Harold Brown Collection

A long line of German POW's clogs an Austrian road as Harold Brown and the 202nd Field Artillery Battalion make their way south in May 1945.

"With their side arms, they could keep order among their own troops. And it worked real well."

Harold says the men around him just watched the procession; they didn't take part in any name calling or verbal provocation with the enemy. Everyone just seemed to be in a state of awe at the sight which extended for miles and miles.

"You wondered how they could lose the war with all of those men..." he says. "God...there were *thousands* of them..."

★ ★ ★

It appeared that, finally, the war was nearly over, and Harold had survived thus far with only minor wounds caused by the bullet-driven rock splinters on the hillside outside of Charmes, France. He had made it through the deadly hedgerow country of Normandy, the tense encirclement and near-destruction of German Army Group B at the Falaise Gap, and the rapid Breakout across France when the 202nd Field Artillery Battalion was exposed at the front of the advance with no protection on its flanks.

He had completed over 50 spotter missions while flying low over enemy lines in a fabric covered airplane, survived strafing by enemy and friendly aircraft, helped hold the Allied line during Hitler's Operation NORDWIND, and assisted in breaching both the Maginot and Siegfried Lines.

HOWITZERS, GRASSHOPPERS, AND THE HOLY RIGHT HAND

Harold was out scouting at the front throughout the American push into central Germany, crossed the Rhine River both in an assault boat and on a ponton bridge, and watched as his Battalion's howitzers shelled "The most German of all German cities."

He had viewed firsthand the examples of Nazi atrocities at the Dachau concentration camp, watched as the birthplace of Nazism timidly fell to the Americans, and, in quiet amazement, had observed the hordes of German soldiers who had decided their war was over and were marching in long columns back towards Germany.

Through 10 months of combat, Harold's luck had held out.

★   ★   ★

Except for the eight weeks spent along the 1945 winter line at Guisberg, France, Harold Brown and the Deuce had been on the move nearly every day, closely following the infantry or armor units they were assigned to support. Similarly for Harold, the upcoming seven day period of May 2 to May 9, 1945, was yet another time of changing locales, missions and experiences. As those days unfolded, he would experience what many people would view as somewhat momentous events in the life of an average American GI in World War II.

Whether due to luck, orders, or the serendipity of the moment, Harold Brown was fated to see and do things that very few of the 16 million Americans in uniform during World War II had a chance to experience. He was given opportunities, and he made the most of them.

What those seven days in May of 1945 would leave Harold with were: a strong sense of duty fulfilled; a few "liberated" items to take back to Colorado as a reminder of his contribution to the defeat of fascism; an opportunity to touch *and* make history; and many, many vivid memories.

And now, as Harold Brown approached the picturesque and historic city of Salzburg, Austria, he was about to be assigned his most unique mission of the war, one which would have far-reaching consequences that would not be resolved for nearly 30 years.

U.S. Army Signal Corps

The view of the Alps from the large picture window in Adolf Hitler's Berghof *residence. Harold Brown stood looking out of this window in the first week of May 1945.*

Chapter 20

Raiding Hitler's Dining Room

★ ★ ★ ★ ★ ★ ★ ★

With an exception or two, an *exact* timeline of just when the following events occurred is difficult to firmly establish. With Adolf Hitler dead, the Russian flag flying over the blackened shell of the Reichstag in Berlin, and the long-awaited disintegration of organized German resistance, daily events on the European battlefronts were progressing rapidly.

For many GI's, the focus of these last few days of conflict shifted from being concerned with defeating a once-determined enemy, to instead being focused on claiming the spoils of war, be they pistols, trinkets or cities. The American soldiers in Europe no doubt felt the weight of a heavy veil lifting, and they began celebrating the fact that they had survived the most destructive, lethal and far-reaching conflict in human history.

HOWITZERS, GRASSHOPPERS, AND THE HOLY RIGHT HAND

Things happened quickly during these last days of World War II, and like many others, Harold was swept along by developments as they unfolded.

From his memory of the events, and from the known facts of what transpired in and around Salzburg, Austria, from May 2 to May 9, 1945, what follows is a likely sequence of incidents, episodes and happenings as experienced by Captain Harold Brown, 202nd Field Artillery Battalion, United States Army.

✯   ✯   ✯

The Allied high command expected the GI's of the 3rd Infantry Division to meet fierce resistance on the approach to Salzburg, Austria.[1]

Well known to the world as the birthplace of composer Wolfgang Amadeus Mozart, Salzburg was also known to the Allies as the city nearest to the Nazi enclave of Berchtesgaden. This quaint alpine village, 15 miles to the south of Salzburg, was where the most important and influential members of the Nazi party had residences. Located on the side of Kehlstein Mountain was the *Berghof*, Hitler's personal residence in Berchtesgaden. Over the years there, he had entertained important officials, planned war strategies, and relaxed with his entourage of fanatical supporters.

A visual highpoint of the structure's design was an enormous plate glass widow that looked out over the steep

Photograph by Third Signal Company.   Courtesy of dogfacesoldiers.org

Downtown Salzburg, Austria, as it appeared when the Americans arrived in May 1945. The Hohensalzburg Fortress, built in the 11th century, commands the historic city from its hilltop perch.

mountainside, affording the viewer a sweeping panorama of the snow-capped Alps. It was an idyllic setting, and a grand prize for the army that could capture it.

★   ★   ★

The 7th Infantry Regiment of the U.S. 3rd Infantry Division was assigned the task of taking Salzburg, and just by chance Harold and the Deuce were assigned by XV Corps HQ to the same area.

The men of the 3rd ID had experienced the tough, bitter fight for Nuremberg, and then the relatively easy occupation of Munich. They had been told, however, to expect a strong defense of Salzburg, but the hordes of German POW's streaming up the autobahn led them to feel otherwise...and they were right.

The 90 miles between Munich and Salzburg were covered quickly and with little resistance. The city itself was undefended, and by the evening of May 3rd, Salzburg was in the hands of the GI's of the 7th Infantry Regiment (IR), 3rd Infantry Division. They had arrived ahead of schedule, and intact as a combat force due to the lack of German resistance.[2]

As the Regiment was fully capable of fighting effectively, quite understandably the commanding general of the 3rd Infantry Division, Maj. General John W. "Iron Mike"

Photograph by Third Signal Company.   Courtesy of dogfacesoldiers.org

Major General John W. "Iron Mike" O'Daniel,
(2nd from left in photograph)
Commander of the U.S. 3rd Infantry Division.

O'Daniel, requested permission from the American command staff to allow the 7th IR to take Berchtesgaden.

General Eisenhower, however, always mindful of the politics that are played out among foreign allies as well as staff officers of the same army, had decided that the glory of capturing Hitler's mountain retreat would go to either the paratroopers of the American 101st Airborne Division, or the soldiers of General Phillipe Leclerc's French 2nd Armored Division.[3] Iron Mike's request was denied.

It appeared that the decision had been made, but the hard-fighting GI's of the 3rd Infantry Division were as equally deserving of the prize of Berchtesgaden as were the American paratroopers and the French tankers. This in no way is meant to imply that the courageous men of either the 101st Airborne or the French 2nd Armor were undeserving of the right to capture the city. But the 7th Regiment of the 3rd ID just happened to be in the area, and they, too, had paid the price in blood to earn the right to take Berchtesgaden.

The 3rd ID had been in action since Operation TORCH, the Allied invasion of North Africa in November 1942. In July of 1943 they invaded Sicily, then the Italian mainland itself. After months of slogging up the Italian boot, the 3rd ID was landed behind the German lines at Anzio, where due to poor planning and intelligence, the American forces were nearly driven back into the blue waters of the Mediterranean Sea. After eventually fighting their way out of the Anzio beachhead, in August of 1944 the 3rd ID was withdrawn from Italy and came ashore in the south of France during Operation DRAGOON. They then spearheaded General Patch's Seventh Army drive to link up with the Allied forces that had come ashore in Normandy.

The men of the 3rd Infantry Division had contributed as much as anyone to the winning of the war, and their commanding general meant to reward them for it.

On the morning of May 4, 1945, and despite General Eisenhower's decision, General O'Daniel gave the order to his men: capture Berchtesgaden.[4]

★   ★   ★

As Harold and the men of the 202nd Field Artillery Battalion moved in and set up quarters in Obertrum, a small mountain town north of Salzburg, the combat patrols from the 7th Infantry Regiment headed south, hoping to be the first Allied soldiers to set foot in Hitler's house.

Expecting to be ambushed by SS troops tasked with the defense of Berchtesgaden, the 7th IR's infantrymen surprisingly met only limited resistance along the way, and by late afternoon U.S jeeps and trucks rolled unmolested into the town square. The GI's quickly rounded up the resident Germans, who seemed to be waiting for the arrival of the Americans, and set about exploring the town.[5]

HOWITZERS, GRASSHOPPERS, AND THE HOLY RIGHT HAND

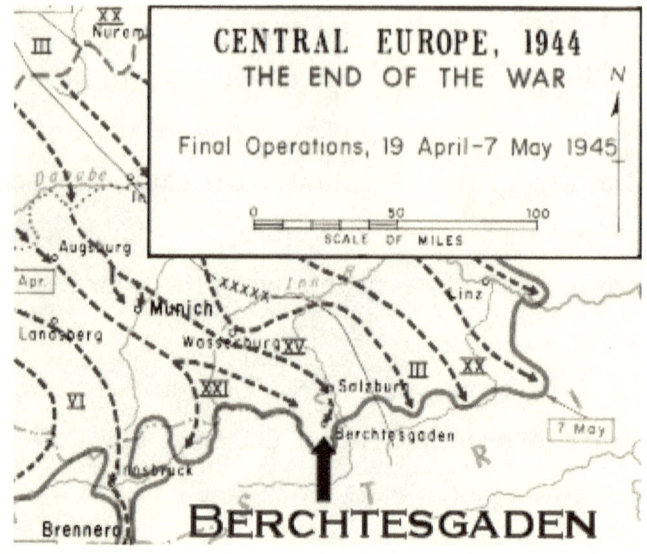

United States Army

A visit to Berchtesgaden, the Nazi mountain enclave south of Salzburg, Austria, would provide Harold Brown with one of his most memorable experiences of the war.

While most of the men busied themselves with exploring the buildings in Berchtesgaden proper, a few of the GI's decided to drive out to the site of the Berghof. The British R.A.F. had bombed Hitler's house and the surrounding structures 10 days earlier, and as a result of this pounding, the buildings and the grounds were in pretty bad shape.[6] Nonetheless, there were still mementos to be found, and everyone was aware that what they didn't take, those who followed behind, would.

Harold Brown was one of those who followed behind.

☆   ☆   ☆

In establishing the timeframe when Harold arrived at the Berghof, it *is* known that early the next morning of May 5th, the men of the 101st Airborne and French 2nd Armor were swarming all over the town of Berchtesgaden.

From Harold's account of his visit to Hitler's house, he arrived there before May 5th; most likely late in the day of May 4th. He and his driver, David Mudge of HQ Battery, had decided to go out and "scout" the Berghof.

"I told Mudge, my jeep driver, 'Let's take a run up to the top of the mountain, if we can get up it, and see what's there,'" Harold recalls. "At that time I didn't have any other responsibilities, so we wound around on the roads, trying to find a way up."

Photograph by Third Signal Company. Courtesy of dogfacesoldiers.org

Adolf Hitler's Berghof residence on the side of Kehlstein Mountain, outside of Berchtesgaden, Austria. The structure exhibits the heavy damage inflicted by British bombs and American artillery. Beyond the house is the view of the Alps that reminded Harold Brown of the Rocky Mountains back in Colorado.

RAIDING HITLER'S DINING ROOM

"It was quite a climb to get there, but we made it up without any detours. We didn't go through the town of Berchtesgaden itself, but ended up close to the Berghof."

They pulled up outside of Hitler's compound, and decided on the best route in.

"Due to the bomb craters, we had to park the jeep," Harold says, "then we walked maybe two hundred yards up to the house."

"The place was deserted; we didn't see any Germans, neither dead nor alive. The house itself was battered…it was in pretty bad shape, and we couldn't find an easy way in."

"Finally we found a side door on the ground level that was open, and we went in there, which was underneath the main floor."

Once inside the Berghof, Harold and Mudge picked their way through the debris and found the stairs leading up to the main living area.

"Then we went up into the large room where you look out that big window over the Alps…what a view!" Harold continues. "Next we went into the kitchen, and then into the dining area where the liquor was stored."

"We came to a liquor room that was clear full of liquor, probably a carload of bottles in there, and lying around the dining room were table settings and everything."

"Unfortunately, we had to get back…couldn't stay too long. So I took a drawer out of a chiffonier there and picked up eight linen napkins from a stack on Hitler's dining room

Photograph by Third Signal Company. Courtesy of dogfacesoldiers.org

This is the view of the Berghof *that Harold Brown and David Mudge had as they walked up to Hitler's house on May 4, 1945.*

Photograph courtesy of Rich Heller warfoto.com

The huge picture window in Hitler's Berghof residence. Harold Brown stood inside the house and looked out through the window opening, marveling at the beautiful view it afforded of the Austrian Alps.

table and laid them in the bottom of the drawer. Then I filled the rest of the drawer with various kinds of liquor, all stamped with 'Reserved for the Wehrmacht.'"

Harold's looting wasn't quite over, however.

"On the way out of the dining room I spotted a little china cream pitcher sitting on the table, so I just took that as a souvenir," he says. "And I still have it."

Believe it or not, Hitler's cloth napkins and china cream pitcher are the only items that Harold "liberated" during his service in World War II.

"That was the extent of my loot; I didn't go in much for loot," he says. "Looting was supposed to be a forbidden thing, you know. But we couldn't keep these guys from doing it, when they were going through fighting. If they saw something they wanted, they took it."

"There were guys who went so far as to take a set of dishes when the going was easy and put it in their pack. This was before the war was over, so the first thing they did when they got into a firefight was to dump the loot! If you got into a rifle fight with the Germans, why, you don't need that load of dishes on your back!"

"There was a lot of that stuff lying in the ditches along the sides of the roads," he says, laughing. "So we tried to discourage that as best as we could."

★ ★ ★

The easy availability of liquor, place settings and other "trophies" places Harold and Mudge at Hitler's house on the evening of May 4th. Another aspect of their visit makes that date seem likely as well:

"On our way up there we didn't have any heavy traffic," Harold says. "We had free access to the roads. Once we got to the Berghof, there weren't many other people there at all; just a few GI's running around."

"And I know we were there before the French…I would have recognized them. Mudge and I just had a cursory examination of the house, spent about an hour there, and then we took off. I'm sure that the 101st came in after we were there, and the French too."

That the Screaming Eagles and French 2nd Armored arrived after Harold's visit was borne out the next morning.

"We went back up a day later to get more of that liquor," he says, "and it was all gone. Somebody had come in after we left and cleared it all out."

"There were hundreds of people there, from all kinds of units, and all along the road there was a whole string of traffic heading up to see Hitler's house."

☆ ☆ ☆

There has been some controversy as to which division actually liberated Berchtesgaden and the Berghof. As the 7th Infantry Regiment of the 3rd Infantry Division was under very strict orders not to loot, many buildings lay untouched after they were ordered back to Salzburg.[7]

When the paratroopers of the 101st Airborne arrived in Berchtesgaden the morning of May 5th and found the town's buildings full of potential "loot", they naturally assumed that they were the first GI's to arrive there, and they claimed the town as captured by their division.[8]

Also adding to the confusion of "who captured what" is the capturing of the Nazi-built structure known as the Eagle's Nest. Not to be confused with the Berghof, the Eagle's Nest was also constructed for use by Hitler, and is located above the Berghof at the top of Kehlstein Mountain. The Eagle's Nest was most easily reached by an elevator shaft inside the mountain, but the power for the elevator was knocked out during the British bombing raid in April. Therefore, a small, winding road had to be traveled to reach the structure. GI's of the 7th IR claim that they, along with the French, climbed to it first.[9] But when the Screaming Eagles of the 101st Airborne Division reached the Eagle's Nest on May 5, 1945, they believed themselves to be the first Allied soldiers to make the climb up the road.[10]

Harold says he did not go to Hitler's mountaintop retreat, so he doesn't have any information that might help to resolve *that* controversy.

Harold's visit to the Nazi enclave outside of Salzburg does, however, corroborate the claim of the 7th Infantry Regiments GI's: they *were* the first Allied troops to enter Berchtesgaden and the Berghof.

Author's Collection

Harold Brown displays one of Hitler's dinner napkins and the china cream pitcher that he "liberated" from Adolf's dining room in Berchtesgaden, Austria.

Harold has Hitler's dinner napkins and cream pitcher to prove it.

(In his book *Crusade in Europe*, General Dwight D. Eisenhower, Supreme Commander, Allied Expeditionary Forces, writes, "On May 4, the 3d Division of the same corps (he is referring to the XV Corps) captured Berchtesgaden."[11] This further reinforces 7th Infantry Regiment's claim.)

★ ★ ★

After leaving the Berghof, Harold and Mudge returned to the Deuce's bivouac in Obertrum and shared Hitler's booze with their fellow artillerymen.

As orders had not been issued to proceed beyond the Salzburg area, the men of the Deuce were focusing their efforts on making their stay in Obertrum a comfortable one. Located 12 miles north of Salzburg on the shores of an alpine lake, Obertrum was a small, picturesque village. Spring had arrived, and one couldn't help but appreciate the beauty of the surrounding countryside.

The view of the Alps in particular affected Harold. "When I was in Salzburg, and especially when I was looking out that big window in Hitler's house, the snow-capped mountains made me think of home," he remembers. "They reminded me of the Colorado Rockies quite a bit."

Harold may have had thoughts of soaring mountains and of his old home on the family farm, but the war was still on, and he realized that the next day would be yet another day of Army routine, and possibly new orders.

★ ★ ★

Harold Brown didn't know it yet, but he was about to get the chance to spend a little time in another small town 2½ miles away, on a mission unlike any other he had experienced during the war.

U.S. Army Signal Corps

A GI is dwarfed by the stacks of artwork and other valuables that were discovered in this church. As the Allies advanced into Germany and Austria, numerous stashes of stolen loot were discovered hidden throughout the two countries.

Chapter 21

The Holy Right Hand

★ ★ ★ ★ ★ ★ ★ ★

"I was in our headquarters, which was located in a building in Obertrum, and we had a telephone system in there that was hooked up to other units in the area," Harold begins. "One of the phones rang, and the call was for our CO, Lieutenant Colonel Tom Lewis."

"He took the phone, and I didn't pay any attention to it until he says 'Brown, take care of that.'"

"That was his favorite line to use with me...'Brown take care of that!'"

"I had *no* idea what he was talking about, so I said, 'What are we going to take care of?'"

"Now, I really liked him as a CO; he always trusted me to do what I was assigned to do. But he never was very good at passing information on...you had to pump him for it."

"Anyway, he says, 'Oh, the OSS has some treasure up there that they want somebody to help with.'"

"So I said, 'What kind of help will I need?'"

"He says, 'Well, they want some backup in case there's any trouble, so take a few men and their rifles, and go up there.'"

"'Where am I going?' I ask."

"'Mattsee,' he says."

"And those were the extent of my orders."

★   ★   ★

About 14 miles north of Salzburg lay two large lakes, or *Sees* as they are known in Austria. The lakes, which are approximately 5 ½ miles long combined, run roughly from the southwest to the northeast, with lake Obertrumer See in the south, and lake Mattsee in the north. Dividing the two lakes, on a small peninsula that juts out from the southern shore, is the small town of Mattsee.

Tucked away in the rolling green hills of northern Austria, the town was only 10 miles from the German border. The Office of Strategic Services, or OSS, was the wartime intelligence organization for the United States, the precursor to the Central Intelligence Agency.

Harold doesn't know how the OSS ended up in Mattsee, but they had apparently found something of value,

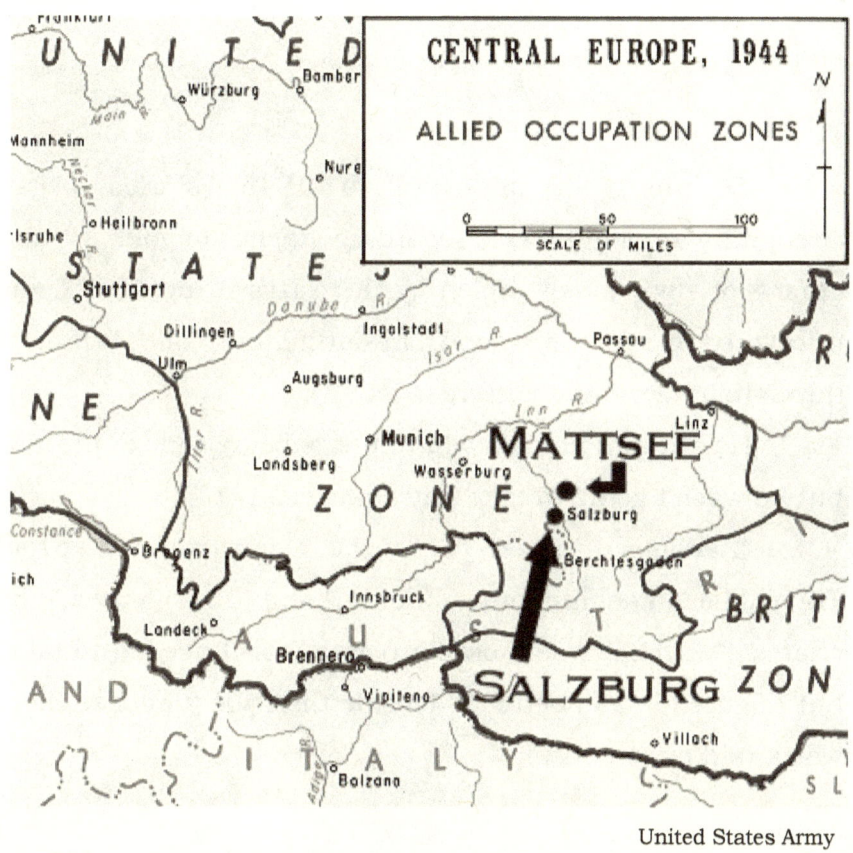

The picturesque lake-side village of Mattsee, Austria, was the site of Harold Brown's final mission of World War II.

and wanted some American firepower on hand for protection.

★ ★ ★

Beginning in mid-April of 1945, stories began circulating among the GI's regarding stashes of gold, art and other loot - previously stolen by the Nazi's - that were being uncovered in salt mines, churches and other "safe" locations throughout Germany and Austria.

Harold had no idea what he was being sent to protect, but he wasn't going to take any chances.

"I arranged to take two of the ¾ ton trucks that had .50 caliber machine gun mounts, and 15 riflemen," he relates. "Maybe it was more firepower than I needed to take, but I figured it was better to be safe than sorry in case there was a raid or something."

By the time he had completed his preparations and the men had drawn ammo and rations, Harold decided it was too late to head out. Just in case there was trouble, he would wait for daylight before making the trip. Therefore, on the following morning of May 6, 1945, Harold and his detail, comprised of 15 artillerymen with rifles, loaded into the two trucks and headed north out of Obertrum.

There had been no further communication from the OSS, so the exact nature of Harold's mission was still vague. But he felt he was as prepared as he could possibly be.

U.S. Army Signal Corps

A Nazi horde of currency and precious metals discovered in an Austrian mine at the end of the war.

U.S. Army Signal Corps

GI's display a piece of recovered art that had been stolen by the Nazi's and hidden in a mine.

THE HOLY RIGHT HAND

Harold hoped he and his men wouldn't run into any trouble, not this late in the war.

Fortunately, the drive to Mattsee was uneventful, and after winding their way up along the lakeshore, the two trucks slowly pulled into the town. Harold then set about trying to find whatever it was he was supposed to protect.

"It was a small town...it just looked like a small German town to me," he recalls. "With the nearby lakes and mountains, it looked like a real nice place."

"We drove around the town briefly until we came upon the church, where out in front there were a few people waiting for us."

"They were the OSS men," he continues, "and with them, looking mighty agitated, was a man in a foreign uniform. He was pacing back and forth in the grass, and you could tell he was pretty upset about something."

"Anyway, I got out of the truck and asked the OSS guys what they wanted me to do. They said the treasure was in the local priest's house, and they wanted me and my men to protect against any trouble."

"I went back to the trucks and told the men what we were going to do, then we drove the trucks across the street to the priest's residence."

"Next I gave the order to deploy, and we set up a defensive perimeter around the house. Just the sight of my men with their rifles seemed to keep people away who didn't belong there, so from what I could tell the townspeople just went on with their usual business."

"The OSS men next asked me to follow them into the house. The priest was there, and he led us into a bedroom on the main floor..."

"...and there in the middle of the room was a big, regular-looking, rough wood shipping crate, about four feet tall, four feet wide, and eight feet long, with metal strapping bands around it; nothing fancy about it."

"We're all standing there looking at it when one of the OSS men said 'We're going to open this crate and examine the contents.' So they broke the metal straps, then one of them took a crowbar and began prying the top off because it was nailed shut."

"Once he loosened it all the way around, they lifted the lid off...and we saw that the crate was filled with *all kinds* of stuff."

"The first thing I noticed was the Crown...there was that Crown sitting there...gold...jewels on it. It was sitting there loose, and it was in great shape...except it had a cross on the top that was bent over."

Harold was looking upon the Holy Crown of Hungary, made in the 12th century...and part of the Hungarian Crown Jewels.

Harold continues with the description of the contents of the crate: "And a whole bunch of clothing...coronation robes were in there. There was a lot of other miscellaneous stuff, but my attention was focused on the Crown..."

U.S. Army Signal Corps

The Holy Crown of Hungary as photographed by the U.S. Army in 1945. The cross atop the crown is clearly bent, just as Harold Brown described it.

HOWITZERS, GRASSHOPPERS, AND THE HOLY RIGHT HAND

"...and the Hand. The Hand was lying there, too, right on top of the coronation robes." Harold grabs his hand at the wrist, demonstrating how big the Hand section was, and the position it was in.

"It was a human hand," he explains, "enclosed in a glass carrier, and it had all of these jewels around it...rubies and pearls and emeralds. It had a piece of ivory, if I remember it right, that it was gripping."

"I picked the glass carrier up and looked it over...it was fascinating."

What Harold was holding in his hands was a piece of sacred history, and one of the most revered religious objects for the nation of Hungary: The Hand of Saint Stephen, also known as the Holy Right Hand.

★   ★   ★

At the beginning of the 11th Century, Saint Stephen was king of what would soon become the nation of Hungary, and it was he who was responsible for bringing Christianity to the various pagan tribes inhabiting that part of Europe.

During Saint Stephen's reign the nation was formally established, and as he played such an important role in the founding of Hungary, shortly after his death it was decided to preserve his right arm, which according to contemporary accounts had not decomposed along with the rest of his body. The Hungarian people took this as a sign from God, and as a result, his right arm was mummified, and

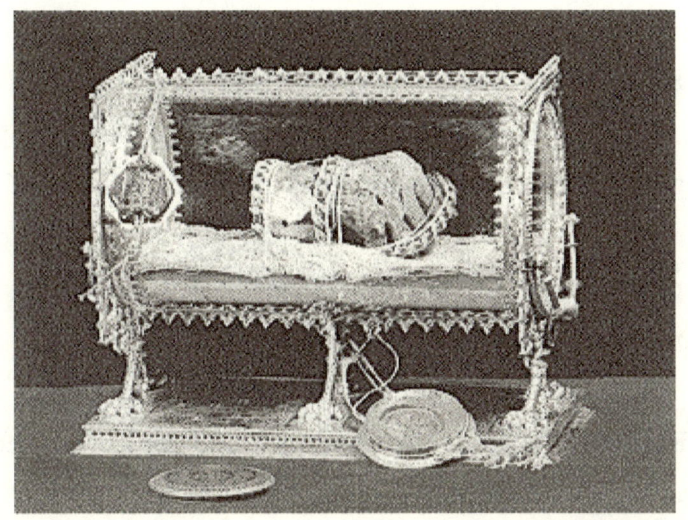

Author's Collection

The Holy Right Hand, encased in the glass carrier that Harold Brown held in Mattsee, Austria.

eventually divided into three pieces, each section sent to a church to be kept as a religious icon and relic.

Of the three sections of Saint Stephen's right arm, the Holy Right Hand is considered the most sacred, and at the onset of World War II it resided in the Hungarian capital of Budapest. During the war, however, Hungary had allied itself with the Nazi's, so as the Russian Army approached Budapest in 1944, the Holy Right Hand was sent to the Archbishop of Salzburg for safekeeping.[12]

Though the exact details of what happened to the Holy Right Hand after it arrived in Salzburg are unknown, it can be safely assumed that the Archbishop sent it to the tiny town of Mattsee, in hopes of preventing it from being stolen or lost forever to the people of Hungary.

Harold and his 15 GI's were there to make sure that didn't happen.

★   ★   ★

The Holy Right Hand and the Holy Crown of Hungary had been placed in the shipping crate, cushioned by the centuries-old Coronation Robes.

"We continued to look at the contents of the case," Harold continues. "Beneath the Coronation Robes were a fancy sword, and a bunch of table settings; they were the Coronation Scepter and the Royal Silver as I found out later.

THE HOLY RIGHT HAND

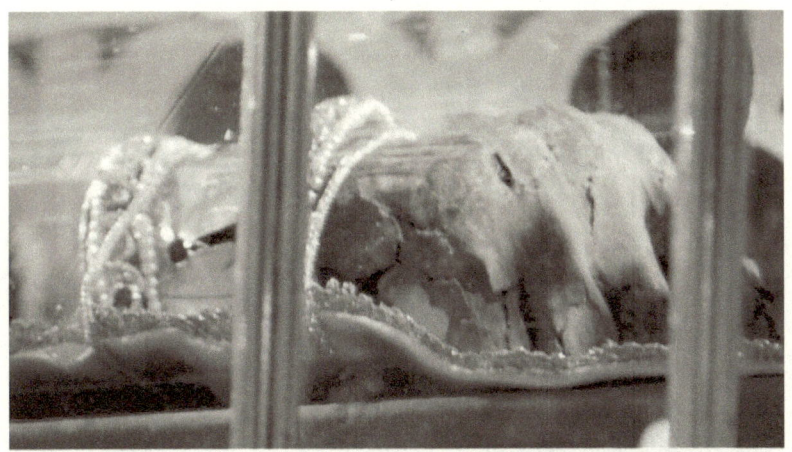

Courtesy of CuriousExpeditions.com

The Holy Right Hand, wearing the precious stone and pearl bracelets that Harold Brown saw in May 1945.

HOWITZERS, GRASSHOPPERS, AND THE HOLY RIGHT HAND

Courtesy of CuriousExpeditions.com

Another view of the Holy Right Hand.

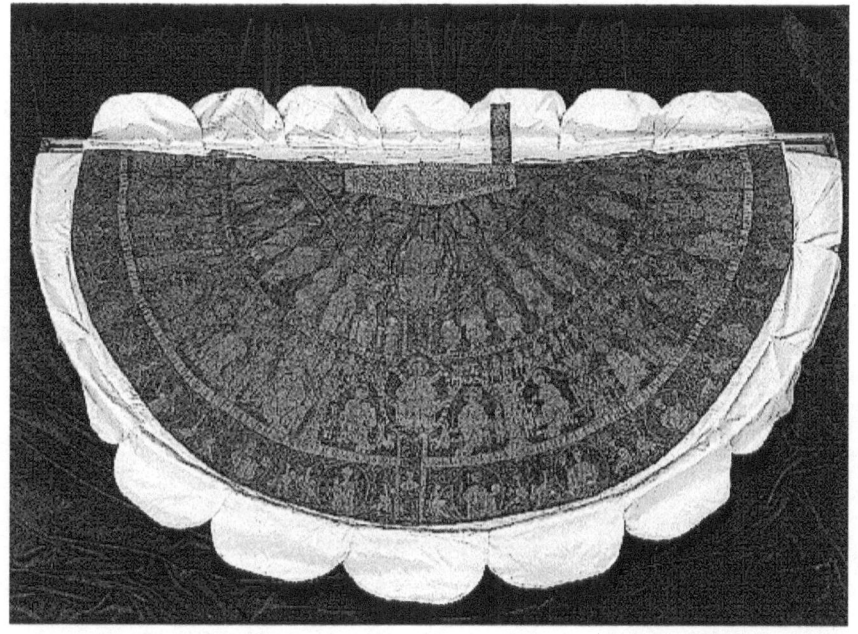

Author's Collection

The Hungarian Coronation Robe on which Harold Brown found the Holy Right Hand and the Holy Crown of Hungary.

We didn't dig down too deep, because we were all surprised at what we had found."

"But the priest just about went crazy when he saw that Hand. He was *really* excited, because he knew what it was! I didn't know what it was...the others didn't know what it was. But it had a religious significance to him that made him want to do something about it."

"He insisted that we take the Hand and set it on the altar of the church which was across the street. I had to slow him down a little bit though, because I didn't want to split that stuff up and have to put guards all over town to protect it."

"So I went to the OSS guys and said, 'If we let him put the Hand on the altar, can I take over this crate with all this stuff and put it in the church too?' 'Sure,' they answered. So that's what we did".

"That crate was heavy though," Harold recalls, "I think due to the weight of the Royal Silver. It took eight men to lift it and carry it across the street."

"We carried the crate into the church, took the Hand out, and placed it on the altar like the priest wanted. We didn't unpack anything else from the crate, and left it in the church. Then I stationed my guys at the doors, and we guarded the church overnight."

Fortunately, the GI's spent an uneventful night at the church in Mattsee, and the following morning was quiet as well. Though the townspeople were now aware of the reason

THE HOLY RIGHT HAND

for the previous day's commotion, they nonetheless went about their usual business, with some of them entering the church to view the Holy Right Hand.

Thankfully, there were no attempts to steal the relics. Whether due to the presence of Harold and his armed GI's or simply because no one of a thieving mind knew they were there, the Hungarian national treasures now were safe and would be protected from damage or from disappearing forever.

★ ★ ★

"Sometime the next day," Harold recalls, "some other American officers came in to take over possession of the relics. I don't know what unit they were from, but they had orders from Army Headquarters to relieve us, and from that point on I don't know what happened to the crate or its contents."

"We protected it while we were there, though," he states proudly. "We did our job, and nothing was looted from the crate."

When asked if he thought of making off with some of the treasure, such as a Royal Hungarian soup spoon or salad fork, while it was in his care, Harold says it never occurred to him.

"I was there to do a job," he says. "I was amazed by what I saw, but I never thought of taking any of it. I knew the Hand had huge religious significance by the way the priest reacted to it, and I figured the contents of the crate were pretty valuable. As a matter of fact, after we had moved the crate into the church, I met a gentleman who had been outside observing the whole thing. He was dressed quite nicely in a civilian suit, and I asked him if he knew what all of that stuff was worth. He said, 'Oh, about 50 million dollars.' Then he retracted that and said quietly, 'You can't put a price on such a find as this.'"

"I don't know who he was or who he was with, but he seemed to know what was in the crate."

The same knowledge was apparently shared by the nervous, pacing man Harold had observed when he and his detail first arrived at the church in Mattsee.

"I found out later," he explains, "that the agitated man was a Hungarian military officer, nervous at the thought that these Hungarian national treasures might become loot for some treasure-seeking American GI's."

Knowing the immense value of the contents of the crate, it is even more of a testament to Harold Brown's honesty and moral character that nothing, not even so much as a soup spoon or salad fork, was looted from the crate while it was under his control. (As a side note, in August 1945, the Associated Press published an article about the contents of the crate, and stated the value at $75,000,000 in 1945 valuations).

THE HOLY RIGHT HAND

As it was, Harold's responsibilities in Mattsee were completed; he and his men were dismissed. They gathered their gear, loaded everything into the ¾ ton trucks and headed back to Obertrum, not realizing the full importance of what they had just been a part of.

★ ★ ★

Upon arriving back at the Deuce's HQ in Obertrum, Harold went inside to see his CO, Lieutenant Colonel Lewis.

"I reported to the Colonel what I had found, and told him that the Army had sent somebody else in to take care of it. We had accomplished our mission, so we came back."

And that was the end of it....for the present time at least.

Throughout the coming months, Harold would occasionally recall the events of May 6, 1945, but it would be another 30 years before his participation in that day's discoveries would be thrust back to the forefront of his mind.

★ ★ ★

For the time being though, on May 7, 1945, Harold had a more mundane, but highly anticipated, event on his mind.

"The building we were bivouacked in was a big house in Obertrum," he relates. "Inside it had a real nice, big bathtub in it, and it had a water heater."

You know where this story is headed!

"Under the heater you lit some wood to heat the water...so I enjoyed a *good...soaking... bath!*" he says with a big, big smile, and you can see in his face just how good that bath must have felt.

"Well, we'd been washing out of our helmets for months...you're taking a bath out of your *helmet!*" he explains.

An event many human beings take for granted, but for Harold Brown and many American GI's in World War II, the opportunity to take a hot bath was one of the greatest things in the world.

★   ★   ★

For Harold, the warm bath in Obertrum ranks up there as one of his fondest wartime experiences. Even though his time in Europe was marked predominantly by the trials and horrors of war, Harold managed to take with him a few pleasant memories.

Foremost would be the many fine men with whom he served in the Deuce-O-Deuce; their shared triumphs, and miseries, would remain with Harold all of his life.

U.S. Army Signal Corps

United States Army personnel bathing out of their helmets. As Harold Brown relates, for many months of combat the "Steel Pot Bath" was usually the only means of washing. The process was made even more difficult in the cold of winter.

He could not easily forget the thankful civilians they encountered in recently-liberated towns, joyous and tearful people who were so grateful to have their freedom restored.

Eating fresh German bread and butter in a farmhouse near the Rhine was another gratifying memory, as was watching General George Patton "standing there like a goof, waving us on," during the race for Paris.

And of course, he would never forget the contents of the crate in Mattsee.

All were good memories, salvaged from the war's dark days that were usually defined by fear, death and destruction, and Harold would reflect on these positive events throughout the coming years.

Of greatest importance to Harold's future, though, were the events of May 8, 1945.

Image courtesy of dogfacesoldiers.org

<u>*The Stars And Stripes*</u> *publishes the official word.*

Chapter 22

Victory in Europe
Farewell to the Deuce

★ ★ ★ ★ ★ ★ ★ ★

"It just came over the wire," Harold says. "I suppose it came down from XV Corps Headquarters."

★ ★ ★

On the morning of May 7, 1945, while Harold and his men were still at Mattsee guarding the OSS's "treasure", 540 miles away in the city of Reims in northeastern France, representatives of Nazi Germany were signing the documents of unconditional surrender, officially ending nearly six years of war in Europe.

The governments of Britain, the Soviet Union and the United States agreed to make the official announcement on the following day.

HOWITZERS, GRASSHOPPERS, AND THE HOLY RIGHT HAND

In 24 hours, World War II in Europe would be over.

★　　★　　★

The phone rang in the Deuce's HQ on the afternoon of May 8, 1945. After 311 days of combat, Harold and the men of the 202nd Field Artillery Battalion heard via a simple telephone call that the war in Europe was over.

So how did he feel when he got the message that the war had finally ended? Harold is somewhat reserved in his response.

"Why, you feel good," he says. "But you're still cautious because there are thousands of German soldiers around you...but fortunately they weren't causing any trouble."

For Harold, there weren't any shouts of joy or dancing in the street at the news that hostilities had officially ended. Did his fellow GI's react differently?

"The men reacted pretty much the same way," he recalls. "You see, we could tell over the past few weeks that the war was almost over...we knew it was just a matter of time."

Certainly, though, the official announcement that the killing had finally come to an end must have had *some* effect. Wasn't there at least a little relief in that? "*Oh yeah...*" Harold says, in a voice that almost has a hint of 60-year-old exhaustion to it.

VICTORY IN EUROPE, FAREWELL TO THE DEUCE

And he leaves it at that.

★   ★   ★

The summer months after the surrender were very busy for the American troops in Germany and Austria as the GI's switched roles from a combat infantry force to an occupation force. Tens of thousands of German soldiers had to be disarmed and processed, then sent on their way home, to a POW camp or, if suspicions arose, held for investigations of war crimes.

Law and order had to be established and maintained, and food, clothing and medical supplies needed to be distributed among the millions of affected civilians in Europe.

The task was enormous in scope, and many units found themselves participating in the occupation process.

Across the globe, however, the war with Japan was still raging, and various European-based units were notified of pending redeployment to the Pacific. The invasion of the Japanese Home Islands was scheduled for November of 1945, and many units currently in Europe would be needed for the bloody fight that was envisioned by the military planners. As fate would have it, the 202nd Field Artillery Battalion was called up for participation.

HOWITZERS, GRASSHOPPERS, AND THE HOLY RIGHT HAND

One day in late July 1945, Captain Brown was called in to Lieutenant Colonel Tom Lewis' office. Harold's CO had a proposition for him.

"The Colonel said he'd get a promotion for me if I'd go with him to Japan," Harold recalls. "He'd see that I was promoted to Major.

"But I told him, 'Give the promotion to somebody else...I've had enough of this.'"

Harold would not be going to the Pacific.

He had seen enough of war.

★ ★ ★

After Harold's decision to turn down the promotion, Lieutenant Colonel Lewis arranged for Harold to be transferred to an artillery battalion that was due to be rotated back to the United States.

Before the Deuce's CO signed-off on the transfer paperwork, however, he made sure to recommend Harold for the Bronze Star and the Air Medal.

On the Bronze Star Citation Lieutenant Colonel Lewis wrote:

VICTORY IN EUROPE, FAREWELL TO THE DEUCE

"Harold E. Brown, Captain, Field Artillery, Headquarters, 202nd Field Artillery Battalion, United States Army, for meritorious service in connection with military operations against an enemy of the United States during the period 2 July 1944 to 9 May 1945. Captain Brown's constant reconnaissance for routes, possible locations for observation posts and forward gun positions many times took him into areas of extreme danger. His keen appreciation of terrain, knowledge of military tactics and cool courage enabled him to select and establish the most advantageous locations for observation into enemy territory. On many occasions Captain Brown personally manned these observation posts and directed devastating fire on enemy personnel and installations while he himself was being subjected to artillery and small arms fire. His leadership, military bearing and strict self-discipline was an inspiring example to all personnel in his organization."

The citation for the Air Medal was similar, reading:

"...for meritorious achievement while participating in aerial flights consisting of thirty-five (35) front line battlefield sorties during the period 2 July 1944 to 4 October 1944. The thirty-five sorties consist of the following:
16 Front line reconnaissances of at least one hour duration.
10 Adjustments of artillery fire in enemy territory.
6 Adjustments of artillery fire on enemy installations.
3 Surveillances of artillery fire on enemy installations.

These flights were made in the vicinities of La Haye du Puits, Carentan, Le Mans, Nantes and Luneville, France, during the campaigns of Normandy and Northern France. As a result of these flights, useful enemy information was obtained and artillery fire was adjusted on the enemy.

Signed,

Tom Lewis
Lieutenant Colonel, Field Artillery
Commanding

★   ★   ★

As the 202nd Field Artillery Battalion prepared for a move north from Obertrum, Harold thanked Lieutenant Colonel Lewis for his efforts as the Deuce's CO, and then expressed his gratitude to the other officers of Battalion HQ. He then bid a final farewell to the men of the Deuce; men with whom he had served through so many experiences - good, bad and miserable - the last 3 ½ years.

VICTORY IN EUROPE, FAREWELL TO THE DEUCE

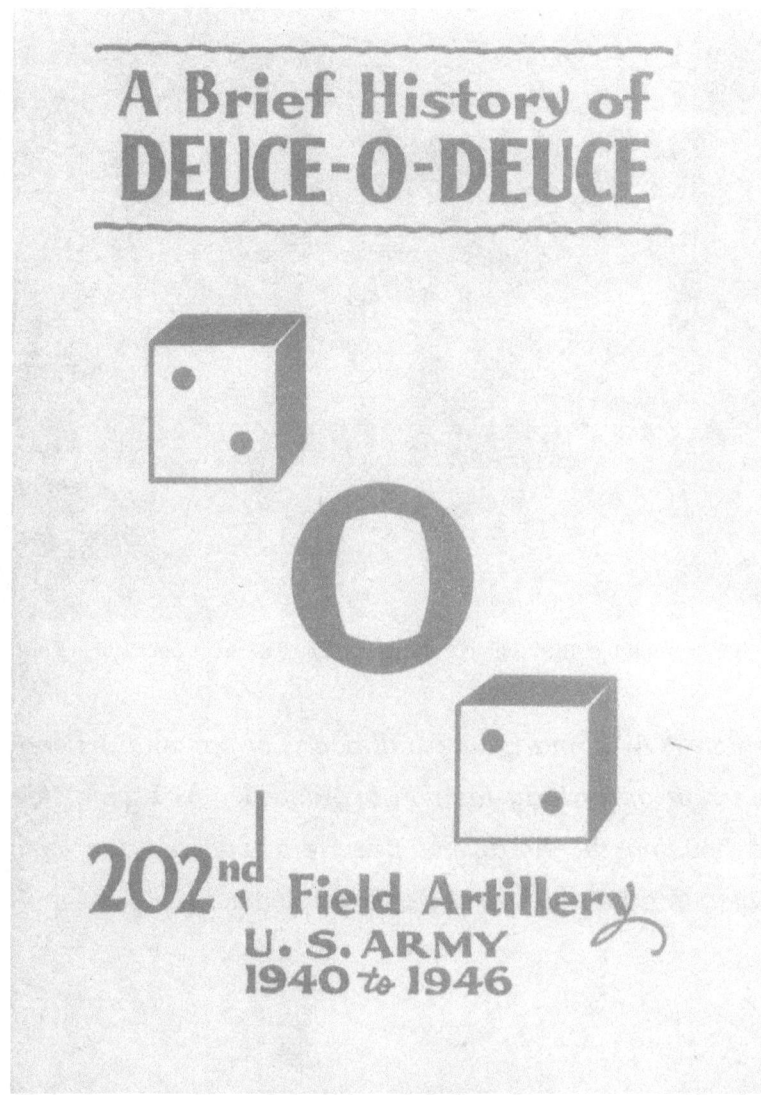

Harold Brown Collection

The cover of the Deuce's Unit History.

Photograph by Third Signal Company.   Courtesy of dogfacesoldiers.org

German POW's, many with full packs of personal belongings, line up in an orderly fashion in Austria. Processing, feeding and housing the hordes of prisoners was a huge logistical problem for the Allies at the end of the war.

Chapter 23

Of Latrine Canvas & Cigarette Camps

★ ★ ★ ★ ★ ★ ★ ★

Shortly after Harold had said goodbye to his friends in the Deuce, the news was flashed around the globe that the Japanese had surrendered.

The Second World War, the most destructive and deadly conflict in human history, had ended, and the peoples of the affected countries began to pick up the pieces, attempting to rebuild their lives.

For the millions of American GI's stationed overseas, the thought of going home and picking up *their* interrupted lives where they had left off was foremost in their minds. Transporting these masses of men and women back to the U.S.A. was a logistical nightmare, however. There simply weren't enough ships available to complete the task quickly.

Not only that, but there were still many vital tasks for the U.S. military to perform, such as the necessary duties of occupation, caring for the millions of displaced persons, establishing civil governments, and disposing of the mountains of military material and supplies that lay scattered throughout Western Europe and the Pacific.

All of this and more remained to be done by the men and women in uniform before they could all expect to be sent home.

★ ★ ★

In order to begin the process of routing American servicemen and women home, and to make it fair to those who had been away the longest, the Army instituted a "points" system. Those individuals with enough points were sent to ports of embarkation to begin the lengthy journey to America.

Points were awarded based on a variety of criteria, such as time spent in combat, awards earned, wounds received, etc. The minimum number of points required for the trip home was 85; Harold had over 100 points.

He wasn't beginning his voyage home quite yet, however...first there were latrines to secure!

★ ★ ★

In June 1945, the artillery battalion Harold was joining was sent from Austria to Landkreis Hilpoltstein, a county in Bavaria, Germany. Harold, being a Captain, was chosen to be the administrator for a town there.

"We were stationed in a real small town outside of Nuremberg, and we were boarded at the schoolhouse," he says. "I guess you can say we had police duties; regulating traffic and the movement of people."

"I had a German schoolteacher with me, a fairly nice looking woman about 35 years old or so, and she could speak perfect English, so I asked her to be my interpreter. She taught in the school where we were staying, but there weren't many students."

The small town was pleasantly quiet, and Harold and his men were occupied mainly with the thousands of travelers who were passing through the town on their way to other destinations.

"When the Germans would come into town and wanted to go on to Munich, they had to have a real good reason to go there or they couldn't proceed as the Army was trying to keep the highways clear," he explains. "To communicate with them I had to rely on the schoolteacher, and I couldn't have done my job without her."

"I got to the point where I could understand what the Germans were asking, but I couldn't answer in German. She did all of the interpreting."

With his interpreter's help, the time Harold spent in the town went smoothly, with one somewhat humorous exception.

"We had a large latrine set up in the town as we had a pretty big group of people there," he begins. "There was an entrance to the latrine, then a canvas wall that wrapped around to where the slit trenches were."

"Anyway, one morning I got up, and the canvas that goes clear around the latrine was gone!"

"So I sat in a stew for about 15 minutes or so, thinking 'What am I going to do about this?'"

"I went to the schoolteacher and asked her if she knew the bürgermeister of the hamlet, and she said she did. I told her, 'You get him down here. I want to talk to him.'"

"Soon she returned with the bürgermeister, and through her I explained to him what had happened."

"Then I told him, 'By tomorrow morning I want that canvas back here, and if it isn't here I'm going to shake down every house in town, one at a time!' I let it go at that...he knew what I meant."

"Then after he left, I thought 'What the heck am I gonna do if he doesn't bring it back?'"

"So I decided to call Battalion Headquarters, and they sent out some ¾ ton trucks with .50 caliber machine guns mounted on them. Once they arrived, we put on an arms show for those people in that town. We paraded the streets all day long with those vehicles with the .50 calibers on them, and it had an effect on the townspeople, I think."

"The next morning," Harold says with a smile, "there was our canvas lying out by the latrine."

The question then begs to be asked, was the latrine canvas so valuable an item that it had to be recovered no matter what?

"It wasn't the value of the daggone canvas," Harold explains, "you just couldn't let them get away with something like that or the next thing you know you are overwhelmed with incidents like that."

☆ ☆ ☆

While he was engaged in the defense of canvas latrine covers in Bavaria in September 1945, Harold finally received word that his orders had come through, and that at long last he was heading home.

It had been over four years since he had left Colorado for Artillery School training at Fort Sill, and the thought of being back with his family was a bit difficult for Harold to comprehend. He had seen and experienced so much in those four years that it was hard to imagine what it would be like to go back to civilian life, to have warm food, warm baths and a warm bed every day. But before he could once again experience those luxuries, he first had to travel the 5120 miles between the small hamlet in Germany and his mother's home in Colorado.

HOWITZERS, GRASSHOPPERS, AND THE HOLY RIGHT HAND

Harold's journey commenced in the type of vehicle that he had ridden in over most of Europe.

"The whole battalion received orders to go to France, and I made the trip in a jeep," he says. "We were ordered to Camp Lucky Strike."

Camp Lucky Strike was one of the nine "cigarette" camps that the U.S. military had set up for staging American GI's on their trip home. Each camp was named after a brand of American cigarettes, and all were located near Le Havre, a French port close to the beaches of Normandy.

Harold says the days he was en route to Camp Lucky Strike are a blur, but from what he recalls, the trip didn't take very long.

"There was just normal traffic on the roads at that point," he says. "I wouldn't say that they were congested at all."

Congestion at the camp was another story, however. The place was teeming with GI's and recently liberated American POW's that were thrilled with being alive and with the thought of going home. The men felt like celebrating, and Harold was chosen to help them do just that.

"They were looking for somebody to go get some liquor from a nearby town, and they picked me to take a truck...I don't know why they picked me, out of all those people!" he says, laughing.

"So I got a 2 ½ ton truck, a driver, and a requisition for liquor, and we went down to the town and loaded that truck clear full as we could load it. Then we drove it back to the camp."

"I guess they knew I wouldn't drink it all! There'd be some of those guys who would have probably tried to distribute it for money. But I got back with it, and it was disbursed out among the troops."

The addition of some liquor added to the cheerful, celebratory atmosphere at the camp, and Harold says the time went quickly.

"I wasn't there very long...seems like it was maybe as short as a week. We weren't keeping track of time or anything, just sort of relaxing...taking it easy until it was time to bid Europe goodbye."

Each day saw hundreds of GI's shipped out of the camp, and hundreds more coming in to take their place. Harold's name was called on October 18, 1945.

"We got shipped out together as a battalion," he recalls. "They broke us up into batteries to keep things organized. I was a battery commander of 125 men or so, and they were all First Sergeants!"

"They had come in from various units, and I thought, 'This is the easiest assignment I've ever had!', because if a guy got to be a First Sergeant, he was a pretty good soldier, you know. He knew how to stay out of trouble. So I felt pretty comfortable with my First Sergeants."

HOWITZERS, GRASSHOPPERS, AND THE HOLY RIGHT HAND

★   ★   ★

Unlike the voyage in the banana boat from Boston to Belfast, where the threat of U-boats and the monstrous waves of the stormy North Atlantic made for a rough crossing, the trip from France to New York City wasn't too bad. The shipboard accommodations were definitely more comfortable: the *S.S Argentina* was a passenger liner that had been converted to a troopship, and though crowded, it beat the banana boat hands-down. If nothing else, the 4000+ GI's onboard the ship had eight days to relax, had time to think about what life would be like when they were finally back home, and, in Harold's case, had an opportunity to visit with acquaintances who were also fortunate enough to have survived the war.

"The ship was loaded with troops, and I met a lot of guys that I had served with in different places," he says.

Of course, with so many servicemen in one place who had a lot of time on their hands, there was a lot of gambling onboard during the voyage. Some things, it seems, never change.

"There were guys who thought of nothing else," Harold states. "Some of the older soldiers that had been in for a long time, it was their main source of fun. When they got paid their $21 a month, they either went home with a pocketful of money, or with empty pockets. They'd gamble their whole month's pay away in about 15 minutes, then say, 'Well, wait 'til next month!'"

National Archives

The passenger liner S.S. Argentina, *which during World War II was converted to a troopship. The* Argentina *brought Harold Brown back to the United States at the conclusion of the war.*

HOWITZERS, GRASSHOPPERS, AND THE HOLY RIGHT HAND

★   ★   ★

It was still daylight on October 25, 1945, when the *S.S. Argentina* drifted past Coney Island, then proceeded into the entrance of New York Harbor. That's when the celebrations started.

"We were all up on the decks for our welcome home," Harold remembers. "We sailed past the Statue of Liberty, and there were all of these little boats running around us, cheering and waving flags at us."

"Once we got to the dock, there was a big crowd of people waiting. Some of the guys on board had family down there. Everyone couldn't wait to get off."

The ecstatic GI's clambered down the gangplanks, some going into the arms of waiting loved ones, most headed to the railway station for the next stage of their journey home.

"We were put on a train to Fort Dix, New Jersey," Harold says. "It was about midnight when we finally got there and unloaded from the train. We lined up on the platform, waiting for somebody to greet us, to tell us what to do next."

"Nobody showed up so we waited and waited. Finally, after standing there for so long doing nothing, my First Sergeant of all the First Sergeants, a guy by the name of Buckmaster, he comes up to me and says, 'Captain, let's do *something* even if its wrong!' He was tired of standing there!"

National Archives

The RMS Queen Mary *arrives in New York harbor, her decks jammed with returning GI's. During the war, the fabled luxury passenger liner was called "The Grey Ghost," a moniker given her due to her wartime paint color, and the fact that she could outrun every German warship and U-boat.*

HOWITZERS, GRASSHOPPERS, AND THE HOLY RIGHT HAND

"But eventually some people came out and started separating us, sending some of us to one place and some to another. It just happened that we hit there in the middle of the night, and when we unloaded off of the train they weren't ready for us."

Another Army SNAFU, but a minor one at this point of the game.

From Fort Dix, the Army made arrangements for sending the GI's to separation centers that were nearest to their hometowns. When Harold's mother sold the family farm after his father died, she had decided to move to Denver in order to gain employment.

"Fort Logan was the closest separation center to Denver, so they gave me a railroad ticket to there," Harold says.

Naturally, the railroads were swamped with military personnel making their way home, and Harold had to wait for a westbound train with an available seat. Luckily, within the day he found a spot, and the train, carrying a mix of civilians and military personnel, pulled out of the station. Harold was homeward bound.

Two days later, he was back in Colorado.

★ ★ ★

Upon arrival in Denver, Harold reported to Fort

OF LATRINE CANVAS & CIGARETTE CAMPS

Logan, and on October 31, 1945, he was put on terminal leave until February 2, 1946, the date when he would be officially separated from active duty with the U.S. Army. Until that date, barring some unforeseen military emergency, he was free to do as he chose.

His paperwork in order, Harold left the main gate at Fort Logan. After 4 ½ years of life in the United States Army, Harold headed into Denver for the homecoming with his mother, and his reunion with civilian life.

CORA N. BROWN
Denver, Colorado.
Entered Air Corps July 10, 1944.
Received training at Fort Des Moines, Iowa August through September 1944.
Served in American Theatre.
Earned Good Conduct and Victory Medal.
Discharged at Fort Sheridan, Illinois.
Date of Discharge: October 1, 1945.
Rank: Private First Class.
Served fourteen months and twenty-one days.
Present occupation is clerk, typist for Colorado Central Power Company, Englewood, Colorado.

Harold Brown Collection

Harold Brown's mother, who did her patriotic duty during World War II.

Chapter 24

Life after War

★ ★ ★ ★ ★ ★ ★ ★

Harold Brown was the eldest of Cora Brown's three sons. Melvin, the middle son, had entered the Marine Corps in July of 1943, and was stationed in the Pacific. Robert, the youngest, joined the war effort as an Army Engineer in April 1945. Therefore, Cora did what any patriotic mother would do: at the age of 48 she volunteered for the United States Army Air Corps! Like many American women in World War II who joined the nation's Armed Forces, Cora Brown was proud to be actively participating in the war effort, especially since all three of her sons were. She was based at Lowry Field in Denver where the Air Corps was training bomber crews, and worked there as a clerk until her discharge on October 1, 1945.

HOWITZERS, GRASSHOPPERS, AND THE HOLY RIGHT HAND

The timing of her separation from military service was perfect: by the end of the month, the first of her boys would be coming home.

★   ★   ★

When Harold began his trip from Europe to the United States, Cora was living in Denver, and it was to her apartment that he went upon leaving Fort Logan.

"She knew I was coming back, but she didn't know when," he relates. "So when I got there, she wasn't home. She had gone out with a friend."

"I got in to her apartment, and I sat down there and waited. Within about a half of an hour or so, here they came...Mom and her friend. I had only seen her three times over the past 4 ½ years..."

Harold was obviously very thankful to be in Colorado again, and no doubt his mother was equally grateful to have her eldest son return home safe and sound.

After spending the first few days catching up on sleep, Harold focused his efforts on assimilating back into society. He hoped for a productive, successful life in post-war America.

★   ★   ★

LIFE AFTER WAR

Harold settled in to civilian life "without any trouble at all," he says. Since he had graduated from college in 1941, he wasn't one of the tens of thousands of servicemen who crowded colleges and universities after the war, making good use of the benefits afforded them by the G.I. Bill. Instead, Harold went straight into the business world.

"I took a job with a life insurance company in Denver, and I sold insurance for about four or five years," he says.

While in Denver, Harold met one Martha Dillner, and in 1950 they were married. They soon started a family, and Harold continued in the insurance business, a profession pursued by many veterans of World War II.

"I did pretty well at it," he states, "but I got tired of it." Harold decided a career change was in order.

"Martha and I had moved to Pueblo, Colorado," he says, "and as my degree was in Agronomy, I had an opportunity to take a position with Moorman's Manufacturing Company out of Quincy, Illinois."

"They produced high-quality feed supplements for livestock, and I worked for them for a while. But then I eventually got into the concrete business in Pueblo where I managed a Ready Mixed company with 25 trucks, and I stayed in that business until I retired."

Harold had adjusted well to civilian life, but after he left active military duty he still felt a responsibility to serve his country.

HOWITZERS, GRASSHOPPERS, AND THE HOLY RIGHT HAND

"I joined the Army Reserve, was promoted to Major, and I stayed in the Artillery until October 1977 when I retired with the rank of Lieutenant Colonel," he says.

✯   ✯   ✯

With successful careers in both business and the military, Harold had done well for himself, his wife and their three children. Occasionally though, he would think back to his time in the war, to the men he knew, the places he traveled through and the sights he saw...especially the gray, withered, bejeweled hand that was encased in glass, and the Hungarian Crown Jewels.

He wondered what ever became of them.

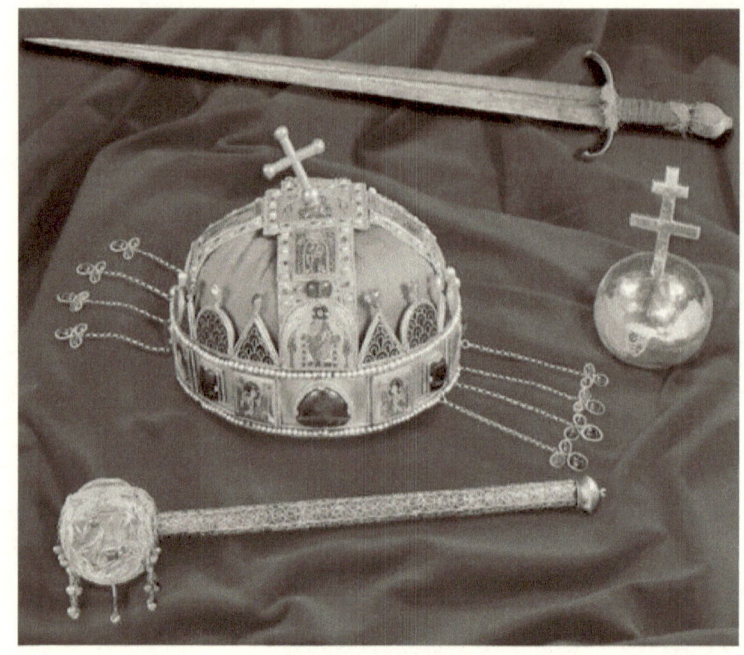

Courtesy of www.CuriousExpeditions.com

The Hungarian Crown Jewels.

Chapter 25

Return of the Crown

★ ★ ★ ★ ★ ★ ★ ★

In late 1977, shortly after retiring from the Army Reserve, Harold came across an article in a local newspaper that thrust him back to his time in Mattsee, Austria when he was a 28-year-old captain in the U.S. Army.

The article stated that, after decades of demands from the communist government of Hungary, President Jimmy Carter had decided to return the Hungarian Crown Jewels to their homeland.[13] This decision set off a storm of protests from displaced Hungarians who did not want to see their national symbols in the hands of a repressive government, the same government that was responsible for calling in Russian tanks to put down the 1956 Freedom Revolution in Hungary.

★ ★ ★

HOWITZERS, GRASSHOPPERS, AND THE HOLY RIGHT HAND

When World War II in Europe ended, the seeds of the Cold War sprouted as Joseph Stalin surrounded the Soviet Union with "satellites", the conquered nations that would form a communist buffer between Mother Russia and the western democracies.[14] Due to fear of this exact scenario, the Hungarian treasures were spirited out of the country in 1944 to keep them from the hands of the Communists.[15]

Shortly after Harold and his guard detail left Mattsee, Austria, in the first week of May 1945, the Hungarian Crown Jewels began a long, circuitous journey, one that would carry them far from Hungary.

In sharp contrast, the Holy Right Hand would begin a relatively short journey that would see it back in the hands of Hungary before the end of the year.

In September 1945, the treasures were taken to the war-torn building that housed the Landesmuseum in Wiesbaden, Germany.[16] Amidst the debris-filled rooms and shattered windows, the American Army laid out and catalogued the vast collection of stolen and misplaced art, precious metals, religious icons and valuables that had been recovered on the wartime drive through Germany and Austria. Over time, many items were restored to their rightful owners. Others, however, holding great political significance, were among the earliest material victims of the Cold War, and their fate would not be decided for many years.

RETURN OF THE CROWN

U.S. Army Signal Corps

The three U.S. Generals nearest the camera (from left), Omar Bradley, George Patton, and Dwight Eisenhower, examine a selection of stolen artwork found in a mine at the end of the war.

As the most important symbols of Hungarian Nationalism,[17] the Hungarian Crown Jewels fell into the latter group. With much secrecy, they were carefully packed up and removed from the Landesmuseum.[18]

The exact details of the journey are not known, but the Crown Jewels eventually ended up in Kentucky, destined to be placed in the high-security vaults of the gold depository at Fort Knox.[19]

There they would remain, for over 30 years.

★   ★   ★

At the end of World War II, the Holy Right Hand was considered a *non-political* relic held sacred by the people of Hungary. As such, on August 20, 1945, St. Stephen's Day in Hungary, a U.S. Army priest gave the glass carrier holding the Holy Right Hand to Bela Witz, the priest of the Hungarian Royal Palace. He carried the relic back to Hungary, where it remains to this day.[20]

For the Hungarian Crown Jewels, the decision of whether or not to return them to their rightful place was not so simple. For many centuries they represented the legitimacy of the Hungarian government. Therefore, in the eyes of the people of Hungary, any governing body that did not have the Crown Jewels bestowed upon it was not recognized as a legitimate government.[21]

RETURN OF THE CROWN

That this was a serious issue for the communist government in Budapest is borne out by the fabrication of a replica crown in 1960's, an attempt by the regime to gain the loyalty of the Hungarian people.[22] This attempt failed, however, and the communist government of Hungary kept up its demands for the return of the relics.

By 1977, the American government was still faced with a difficult political situation in regards to the Hungarian Crown Jewels. At that time, the Soviets still had thousands of troops stationed in Hungary, and the many Hungarians who fled communist rule were adamant that the relics not be handed over to those in the atheistic Hungarian government who they considered to be traitors.[23] [24]

Lawsuits were filed, complaints were lodged, but the course of history was set. President Carter decided that the time had come, and the relics would return to the Hungarian people.

On January 5, 1978, a U.S. Air Force jet took off for Europe, carrying the Hungarian Crown Jewels back to Budapest, the city they had left 34 years prior.[25]

★ ★ ★

The mystery surrounding the finding of the Holy Right Hand and the Hungarian Crown Jewels is a subject that should be revisited.

Similar to the controversy regarding which U.S. Army Division liberated Berchtesgaden and Hitler's Berghof, there is also confusion as to who is responsible for actually finding the Holy Right Hand and Hungarian Crown Jewels. Prior to the publishing of this book, a *detailed* description of how and where the Hand was located did not exist. If such a description does exist, it is not easily located. There are published accounts of how the Crown Jewels ended up in the hands of the U.S. Army, but few of them contain the detail provided by Harold Brown; for the most part, they contain generalities regarding who, what and where. They are worth reviewing, however, as the other accounts contain information that corroborates with Harold's recollections.

One account of the episode begins with the individual who most likely was the "agitated" man Harold Brown saw in Mattsee: Colonel Ernoý Pajtás of the Hungarian Army. He was also the head of the Hungarian Crown Guard, and he and a dozen soldiers with him had sworn to protect the treasures with their lives. They had moved the relics farther and farther from Budapest as the Russians advanced, and on May 2, 1945, they drove to Zellhof, Austria, a Catholic mission estate on the outskirts of Mattsee. With them they had a large chest, locked with three padlocks, and emblazoned with the Hungarian coat-of-arms. They remained at Zellhof for a few days, until, on May 6, 1945, the Catholic priest of the mission drove to nearby Seeham, Austria, to inform American soldiers of the Hungarians' presence. A lieutenant was assigned to check out the priest's claim, and upon arriving at Zellhof, he apparently convinced the Hungarians to surrender. They returned with the lieutenant to Seeham, along with the locked chest.[26]

Another account also centers around Pajtás. In May 1945, the story goes, he brought the chest containing the Crown to Seventh Army Headquarters. The chest was secured by three locks, for which Pajtás claimed he did not have the keys. Somehow the press found out about the chest, and demanded to see the treasures. A few weeks later (June 1945?) the keys were miraculously found, but the chest was empty when opened. Pajtás admitted to hiding the contents of the chest, and he was "persuaded" to retrieve the items (During one of our interviews, Harold Brown described the Hungarian officer as "beat-up around the face"...perhaps as a result of being "persuaded"). Without official authorization, Pajtás was allowed to leave in the dead of night to recover the artifacts. He returned with a mud-covered drum containing the relics. With the assistance of the GI's, the items were washed clean in a bathroom, and then returned to the chest. The press was then allowed to view the treasure.[27]

HOWITZERS, GRASSHOPPERS, AND THE HOLY RIGHT HAND

The following version has a similar storyline. At the end of World War II, the story claims, American GI's apprehended a group of Hungarian SS troops who had in their possession the Crown Jewels' storage boxes, but the boxes were empty. During interrogation, the story continues, the Hungarians admitted that they had placed the Crown, Scepter and Orb in an oil barrel, and then had sunk the barrel in some marshland around Mattsee. GI's of the U.S. Seventh Army eventually located the barrel and recovered the contents.[28]

Yet another account claims that on May 2, 1945, the treasures, contained in a large, black satchel, were given by a Hungarian general to a U.S. Army colonel in Egglesberg, Austria (Egglesberg is 13 miles northwest of Mattsee). The items were sent to Wiesbaden (location of the Landesmuseum), then to Fort Knox.[29]

News reports in August 1945 gave credit for the find to the 42nd Infantry Division. The "Rainbow" Division's History states that at the end of the war, they "guarded the Hungarian Crown Jewels."[30] Taken literally, this could very well be a true statement. As the 42nd ID was stationed in Austria at the time the treasure was found, it is entirely possible that after Harold and his men were dismissed, the GI's of the 42nd ID were assigned to escort the items. By the time they assumed guard duties, the contents of the find were known, and no doubt word spread of the immense value of the items in the plain-looking shipping crate.

Lastly, there is a published account that seems to give the best explanation for why the relics were removed from the royal chest in the first place (and why they may have ended up in the plain, wooden shipping crate that Harold saw). The Nazi-backed leader of Hungary was Prime Minister Ferenc Szálasi. As the war neared its end, he concocted a plan to ensure his return to a position of authority within Hungary. He ordered Colonel Pajtás to remove the treasures from the chest and to hide them. After the locked chest was turned over to the Americans, Szálasi planned on charging the GI's with the theft of the royal artifacts. Then, using the unknowing press to publicize the scheme, Szálasi intended to "discover" the hidden items, thereby making himself a hero in the eyes of the Hungarian people.[31]

★ ★ ★

What are we to make of all of these differing claims surrounding the finding of the Hungarian Crown Jewels? Some of the stories do share similar details, and may have originated from the same original source(s). None of the accounts, however, mention the Holy Right Hand. The few references to the Hand merely state that at the end of the war, it ended up in the possession of the U.S. Army. Yet, the Hand had to have been located by someone. Most of the prior stories provide little detail other than "the Hungarian

Crown Jewels were found." With the dishonesty displayed by Pajtás and Szálasi, their accounts of the events must surely be taken with a grain of salt. Additionally, in regards to the Hand, Harold Brown's recollection of the events of May 6, 1945, offer the only detailed explanation of who, what and where: the OSS had located the relic – Harold never claimed that he did; the crate contained the Holy Right Hand, along with the Holy Crown, the Coronation Scepter and Robes, and the Royal Silver; the items were held in a plain-looking shipping crate that was stored at a priest's house in the tiny village of Mattsee, Austria, a location the Archbishop of Salzburg probably felt was as safe as any.

Throughout their history, the Hungarian Crown Jewels have at various times disappeared, been stolen, or sent abroad. The remarkable thing is that all of the pieces have managed to be reunited, and then returned to their rightful home in Budapest, Hungary. The same holds true for the Holy Right Hand. The artifacts have led a tumultuous but, in the end, blessed life. Certainly *some* credit for the restoration of the Holy and Royal relics to their rightful place belongs to one Captain Harold E. Brown, United States Army Artillery, World War II. Without his honesty, decency and professional dedication, who knows what attic, crate or musty box the treasures might have ended up in, possibly lost to the world for all time?

RETURN OF THE CROWN

★ ★ ★

As of the publishing date of this book, the relics still reside in Budapest, on display for visitors to see.

The Holy Right Hand may be viewed at the Basilica of St. Stephen, where it rests in the glass carrier, safely protected by an ornate reliquary made of gold.

The Hungarian Crown Jewels are on display in the Hungarian Parliament Building, restored to a place of honor in the now-democratic country.

★ ★ ★

After all that has transpired, and with the hindsight afforded by the 60 years since he was in the battlefields of Europe, how does Harold Brown feel about his experience in World War II?

"Well, I feel good about it, you know?" he says. "I think I did my share."

Harold Brown did do his share...

...and *that's* a fact no one can deny.

★ ★ ★ ★ ★ ★ ★ ★

Courtesy of CuriousExpeditions.com

The Reliquary for the Holy Right Hand as it appears in 2007 at Saint Stephens Basilica in Budapest, Hungary.

The Hungarian Crown Jewels on display in 2007 at the Parliament Building in Budapest, Hungary.

ENDNOTES

[1] John C. McManus, "Race to Seize Berchtesgaden," *World War II*, May 2005.

[2] Ibid.

[3] Ibid.

[4] Ibid.

[5] Ibid.

[6] Dwight D. Eisenhower, *Crusade in Europe*, (Garden City, New York: Doubleday, 1948), 420.

[7] John C. McManus, "Race to Seize Berchtesgaden," *World War II*, May 2005.

[8] Major Dick Winters, *Beyond Band of Brothers* (New York: The Berkley Publishing Group, 2006), 218.

[9] www.warfoto.com/berchesg.htm#Truth

[10] Winters, *Beyond Band of Brothers*, 222.

[11] Eisenhower, *Crusade in Europe*, 418.

[12] Lynn H. Nicholas, *The Rape of Europa, The Fate of Europe's Treasures in the Third Reich and the Second World War* (New York: Vintage Books, 1995), 431.

[13] Harold Brown recalls seeing this article in the Pueblo newspaper, but he doesn't remember the exact date.

[14] Henry Luce, "Foreign News - World of Enemies." *Time*, 17 January 1944.

[15] Nicholas, *The Rape of Europa*, 431.

[16] Tibor Glant, "Walter I. Farmer, the Wiesbaden Art Collecting Point and the Holy Crown of Hungary." *Vasváry Collection Newsletter*, Issue 2, 1997.

[17] *The Lawton Constitution.* "Court Action Fails, Crown of St. Stephen to be Returned." January 5, 1978.

[18] Nicholas, *The Rape of Europa,* 432.

[19] *The Lawton Constitution.* "Court Action Fails, Crown of St. Stephen to be Returned." January 5, 1978.

[20] www.historicaltextarchive.com/hungary/hand.html

[21] Buchanan, Patrick. "Hungary Patriots Twice Betrayed." *New York Times News Service.* Publication date unknown as Harold Brown had a photocopy of a news-clipping of this article, although Buchanan writes that "this weekend the United States will deliver the sacred crown of St. Stephen to the Hungarian traitor Janos Kadar..." Therefore, a likely publication date is in the first few days of January 1978.

[22] Ibid.

[23] Ibid

[24] *The Lawton Constitution.* "Court Action Fails, Crown of St. Stephen to be Returned." January 5, 1978.

[25] Ibid.

[26] Kenneth Alford, *Nazi Plunder: Great Treasure Stories of WWII* (Cambridge: De Capo Press, 2001) 137-138.

[27] Nicholas, *The Rape of Europa,* 431.

[28] www.detecting.org.uk/html/hungarian_crown_jewels_nazi_gold.html

[29] http://hungary.usembassy.gov/holy_crown.html

[30] www.42id.army.mil/history

[31] Alford, *Nazi Plunder: Great Treasure Stories of WWII,* 144-145.

BIBLIOGRAPHY

Books

Alford, Kenneth. *Nazi Plunder: Great Treasure Stories of WWII*. Cambridge: De Capo Press, 2001.
Breuer, William. *Operation Dragoon: The Allied Invasion of the South of France*. Novato, CA: Presidio, 1987.
Eisenhower, Dwight. *Crusade in Europe*. New York: Doubleday, 1948.
Nicholas, Lynn. *The Rape of Europa, The Fate of Europe's Treasures in the Third Reich and the Second World War*. New York: Vintage Books, 1995.
Taggart, Donald. *The History of the 3rd Infantry Division in WWII*. Nashville: The Battery Press, 1987.
202nd Field Artillery Battalion. *A Brief History of the Deuce-O-Deuce: 202nd Field Artillery, U.S. Army 1940 to 1946*. Privately printed.
Winters, Richard. *Beyond Band of Brothers: The War Memoirs of Major Dick Winters*. New York: The Berkley Publishing Group, 2006.

Articles

Associated Press. "Court Action Fails, Crown of St. Stephen to be Returned." *The Lawton Constitution*, January 5, 1978.
Ballard, Ted. "Rhineland: The U.S. Army Campaigns of World War II." U.S Army Center of Military History. Publication 72-25.
Cirillo, Roger. "Ardennes-Alsace: The U.S. Army Campaigns of World War II." U.S Army Center of Military History. Publication 72-26.
Buchanan, Patrick. "Hungarian Patriots Twice Betrayed." *New York Times News Service*. Publication date unknown as Harold Brown had a photocopy of a news-clipping of this article, although Buchanan writes that "this weekend the United States will deliver the sacred crown of St. Stephen to the Hungarian traitor Janos Kadar…" Therefore, a likely publication date is in the first few days of January 1978.
Glant, Tibor. "Walter I. Farmer, the Wiesbaden Art Collecting Point and the Holy Crown of Hungary." *Vasváry Collection Newsletter*, Issue 2, 1997.
Illényi, Balázs. "The Adventures of the Holy Crown of Hungary." *The Hungarian Quarterly*, Summer 2000.

Lynn, Katalin Kadar. "The Return of the Crown of St. Stephen and Its Subsequent Impact on the Carter Administration." *East European Quarterly*, Vol. 34, 2000.
Luce, Henry. "Foreign News - World of Enemies." *Time*, 17 January 1944.
McManus, John. "Race to Seize Berchtesgaden." *WWII*, May 2005.

Web Sites

http://hungary.usembassy.gov/holy_crown.html
www.archives.gov
www.curiousexpeditions.org
www.dean.usma.edu
www.detecting.org.uk
www.dogfacesoldiers.org
www.42id.army.mil/history
www.historicaltextarchive.com/hungary/hand.html
www.historicaltextarchive.com/hungary/jewels.html
www.warfoto.com

INDEX

Photographs indicated by page numbers in *italics*

Anzio, Italy	334
Archbishop of Salzburg	360, 410
Argentan, France	117, 118
Audley Hotel (London)	44
B-17 Flying Fortress	140-41
Bad-Kissingen, Germany	275
Belfast, Ireland	37
Berchtesgaden, Austria	330, 334-35, 337, 343-44, 406
Berghof	7, *328*, 330, 337, *338*, 339, *340-41*, 343-44, 346, 406
Berlin, Germany	14, 271-72, 275, 318
Bining, France	182
Boobytraps	95
Boston, Massachusetts	26
Bradley, Omar N.	*100*, 101, 103, *105*, 106, *116*, *403*
Brawley, (British Major)	43
Bricquebec, France	106
Brouvelieures, France	*144*
Brouviller, France	167, 169
Brown, Cora	*394*, 395-96
Brown, Melvin	395
Brown, Robert	395
Brown, Wayne	xxi
Buchenwald, Germany	304
Budapest, Hungary	360, 405-06, 410-11
Caen, France	117
Camp Barkeley, Texas	14
Camp Drumilly, Ireland	37, 41
Camp Howes, Texas	26
Camp Lucky Strike, France	386
Camp Miles Standish, Mass.	26, 29
Carentan, France	4, 90, 103, 106, 378
Carter, Jimmy	401, 405
Central Intelligence Agency	350
Charmes, France	147, 325

Clairefontaine, France 163
Cole, John "Jack" *xix*
Colorado State College of Agriculture and Mechanic Arts 7, 8
Cotentin Peninsula 67, 107

Dachau, Germany *303*, 304, *305*, *307-08*, 311, 326
Danube River 229, *300*
D-Day (June 6, 1944) 3, 57, 63-65
De Gaulle, Charles 129
Denver, Colorado 392-93, 395, 397
Destroyer Escort (DE) 32
Diamond T (truck) 47, 49
Dietrich, Marlene *216*
Dietrich, Sepp 43
Dillner, Martha 397
DRAGOON, Operation 219, 335
DUKW (Amphibious truck) 299, *301*

85th Engineer Heavy Ponton Battalion 245, *246*, 247, *248-49*, 253, 254, 256, *259-60*, 299, *300*
87th Infantry Division 175
88mm (Hedgerow shelling) 84
Eisenhower, Dwight D. 103, *105*, 200, 334-35, 346, *403*
Egglesberg, Austria 408

Falaise Gap (France) 4, 107, 117-18, *121*, 122, 125, 135, 325
XV Corps – U.S. 240, 298, 332, 373
5th Armored Division 107
Flagg, Gurden 148, 150-52
Flaherty, John 136
Fort Collins, Colorado 8
Fort Dix, New Jersey 390, 392
Fort Knox, Kentucky 404, 408
Fort Logan, Colorado 392-93, 396
Fort Sam Houston, Texas 11-13
Fort Sill, Oklahoma 9-12, 385
42nd Infantry Division 299, 302, 312, 408
44th Infantry Division 169, 173, 186, 190, 195
45th Infantry Division 13, 19, 304
Frankenheim, Germany *280*
Frankfurt, Germany 272
French 2nd Armored Division 334, 337, 343

Giannetto, Samuel 28, 29, *134*
Grasshoppers (light aircraft) 20, 92, *93*, 138-39, 157, 166-67, 205, *206*

Greenberg, Shelton   168
Gros-Rederching, France   182, 189
Guisberg, France   199-200, *201*, 205, *208*, 211, 215, 222, 326

Hammelburg, Germany   275
Hand of Saint Stephen – see "Holy Right Hand"
Hardin, "Doc"   *316*
Hathaway, Allen   167
Heller, Rich   xiv
Heller, William (Bill)   xiv, *xvi*, *xix*
Herr, Orris   166
Hitler, Adolf   4, 14, 185-86, 278, 298, 302, *310*, 318, 329-30, 346
Holy Crown of Hungary   356, *357*, 360, *400*
Holy Right Hand   358, *359*, 360, *361-62*, 365, 402, 404, 406, 409-411, *412*
Hornbach, Germany   270
Horsa (glider)   *75*
Hungarian Crown Jewels   398, *400*, 401-02, 404-06, 408-11, *413*

Jagdpanzer 38 (tank destroyer)   *280*
Johanson, Martin   148, 150, 152
Johnstown, Colorado   xxiii, 7, 8
Jones, Merle   84, *86*, 87

Kaiserlautern, Germany   234
Kaylor, U.S. Colonel   49
Kehl, Germany   *235*
Knetzgau, Germany   275, 283
Krouse, Marvin   *197*

La Haye-du-Puits, France   90, 378
Land mines (Normandy)   81
Landkreis Hipoltstein, Germany   383
Le Clerc, Phillipe   334
Le Havre, France   380
Le Mans, France   107, 117, 378
Lewis, Tom   4, 42, 190, 256, 349, 367, 376, 378
Liverpool, England   46
Lohr am Main, Germany   275
Lohr, France   *221*
London, England   42, 44
Lowry Field, Colorado   395
LST (Landing Ship, Tank)   51, *52-53*, 54, 63-64, 67, *68*, 74
Luftwaffe (German Air Force)   4, 44-45, 90, 139
Lunèville, France   162, 378

M1, 155mm Howitzer 15, 50, 77, *80*, 94, *98-99*, 130, *172*, 194, *259*, 286
M-5 Prime Mover, "Cats" 47, *48*, *98-99*, 211, *259*
M7 Self-propelled Howitzer *210*
M8 Scout Car *160*
M10 Tank Destroyer *171*, *187*, *260*
Maginot Line 175, *176-77*, 179, 325
Main River 272, 275, 283
Mattsee, Austria 4, 350, 355, 360, 364, 366-67, 370, 373, 401, 406, 408, 410
McAnally, Hoyt 148, 150, 152-53
Mènil-Flin, France 162
MG-34 (machine gun) 148, *149*, *170*
Mommenheim, France 173
Montgomery, Bernard L. *116*, 117, 122, 128
Mudge, David *134*, 337, 346
Munich, Germany 302, 304, *310*, 311, *313-15*, 318, *320*, 322, 332, 383
Mussolini, Benito *310*
Mutzig, France *231*

Nancy, France 147, 162
Nantes, France 378
961st Field Artillery Regiment 46, 49-50
Nonant-le-Pin, France 118
Nuremberg, Germany 275, 278, *282*, 283, 285-87, *288*, 289, *290-97*, 299, 312, 332

O'Barr, Milt xiv, *xvii*
O'Barr Rod xiv
Obertrum, Austria 335, 346, 349, 352, 367-68, 378
O'Daniel, John W. 332, *333*, 334-35
Omaha Beach 61
100th Infantry Division 180, 186, 190, 195
101st Airborne Division 334, 337, 343-44
189th Field Artillery Regiment 13, 15-16, 19
Order Of Battle School 43
Office of Strategic Services (OSS) 4, 350, 352, 355-56, 364, 373
Ostheim, France *193*
Oothoudt, Otis 194-95, *197*
OVERLORD, Operation 74
Oxford, England 46

P-47 Thunderbolt 244-45
Pajtás, Ernoý 406-07, 409-10
Patch, Alexander M. 155, 157, *159*, 162, 166, 220, 335

Panther tank	73, *111*, 112, *177*
Paris, France	128-29, 130-31, 135, 145, 318
Parmer, Glenn	254, *255*, 256
Patton, George S.	103, *105*, 106-07, *116*, *124*, 126-29, 145, 370, *403*
Pearl Harbor, Hawaii	13
Pecy, France	131
Piper Cub L-4	20
Ponton (pontoons)	245, *246*, 247, *248-49*, *259-60*, 299, *300*, 326
Proximity-Fuze	189-90
Pueblo, Colorado	397
Quonset Huts	38, *39*
Ravenoville, France	69
Reims, France	373
Rhine River	4, 162, 200, 234, *236*, 237, 239-41, 244-45, 247, 250, *251*, 252, 254, 256, *259-60*, 263, 272, 284, 298, 326, 370
Rhone River	220,
Rimling, France	173, 179, 186
Rommel, Erwin	43-44
Roosevelt, Franklin Delano	284-85
Saint-Lô, France	103, *104*
Ste-Mère-Eglise, France	69
Saint Stephen	358, 360
Salzburg, Austria	4, 318, 322, 327, 330, *331*, 332, 335, 344, 346, 350, 360
Saverne Gap, France	162, 166, 169, 173, 185
Schleier, George	167
Schmittviller, France	182, 192
Schweinfurt, Germany	272
Schweizer Hof, Germany	299
Seeham, Austria	407
Seesock, Robert "Bobby"	*xix*
Sennybridge Mountains, Wales	47
Seventh Army – U.S.	155, 157, 167, 180, 185-86, 220, 302, 335, 408
7th Infantry Regiment	332, 334-35, 343-44
17th SS Panzer Grenadier Division	186
79th Infantry Division	129-30, 166
Sherman tank	109, 112, *113-14*, *174*, *214*, 262, 288
Siegfried Line	222, *223-25*, 226, *227*, 229, *230*, *232-33*, 234, 237, 239, 298, 325
6th Armored Division	304
Skulski, Walter	*253*

Snipers	78, 250, 252
Southampton, England	50
Speer, Albert	278, 289
Sperrin Mountains, Ireland	40
S.S. Argentina	388, *389*, 390
Stalin, Joseph	402
Steinach, Germany	*273*
Strasbourg, France	162, *174*
Sturmgeschutz IV	*221*
Szálasi, Ferenc	409-10
Taunton, Massachusetts	26
Third Army	106-107, 117, 145, 157
3rd Infantry Division	*218*, 219, 222, *228*, 235, *235*, 237, 239-41, *242*, 247, *269*, 271, 275, 286-87, 289, 298, 330, 332, 334-35, 343
36th Volksgrenadier Division	186
Thuras, Dylan	xiv
Tiger tank	109, *110*, 112
Toomey, Bill	xv, *xviii, xix*
Toomey, Denis	xiv
TORCH, Operation	334
U-Boat	32-33
Uren, Lester	*197*
Utah Beach	3, 61, 63, 69, *70-71*
Vindefontaine, France	77
Vosges Mountains, France	157, *158*, 162, *198*, 199, *202*, *212*, 220, 298
von Runstedt, Gerd	43
WACO glider	*76*
Wales, U.K.	47
Wheatley, England	46-47, 69
White, John	167-68
Wiesbaden, Germany	402, 408
Witz, Bela	404
Worms, Germany	239, 254
Wörth am Main, Germany	272
Zellhof, Austria	406-07
Zweibrücken, Germany	222, *238*

Harold Brown and the Author

About the Author

Born in the last year of the Baby Boom that followed World War II, John Niesel has had a life-long interest in the decade of the 1940's that shaped the world in which we live today. After attending the funeral for his Great-Uncle Roy Ellinghausen (one of his family's five great-uncles who served during the war) in 2004, Mr. Niesel determined he wanted to take an active role in the preservation of the accomplishments and sacrifices of America's WWII citizen soldiers. In 2005 he founded *Framing History*, a company offering historic art that focuses on the memories of the WWII generation. Mr. Niesel is also a member of the 10th Mountain Division Living History Display Group, and through living history presentations he educates the public on the legacy of Colorado's WWII Ski Troopers, and on the sacrifices of America's WWII servicemen and servicewomen, so they will not be forgotten by future generations. He resides in Colorado with his wife, Julie, and son, Ian.

www.ingramcontent.com/pod-product-compliance
Lightning Source LLC
Chambersburg PA
CBHW032013230426
43671CB00005B/75